ANSWERS TO COMMON
QUESTIONS ABOUT

The End
Times

ANSWERS TO COMMON QUESTIONS ABOUT

The End Times

Timothy J. Demy
Thomas Ice

Kregel
Publications

Answers to Common Questions About the End Times
© 2011 by Timothy J. Demy and Thomas Ice

Portions of this book were previously published by Kregel
Publications as *What the Bible Says About the End Times*.

Published by Kregel Publications, a division of Kregel, Inc.,
P.O. Box 2607, Grand Rapids, MI 49501.

The views expressed in this book are solely those of the authors and do not represent or reflect the position or endorse-
ment of any governmental agency or organization, military
or otherwise.

Library of Congress Cataloging-in-Publication Data
Demy, Timothy J.
  Answers to common questions about the end times /
Timothy J. Demy and Thomas Ice.
    p. cm.
  Includes bibliographical references.
1. End of the world—Miscellanea. I. Ice, Thomas. II. Title.
BT877.D46   2010   236'.9—dc22   2010041561

ISBN 978-0-8254-2658-2

Printed in the United States of America

11 12 13 14 15 / 5 4 3 2 1

Contents

Part 5: What Does the Bible Teach About the Millennium? 104

Part 6: What Does the Bible Teach About Heaven and the Eternal State? 118

About This Series

The Answers to Common Questions series is designed to provide readers a brief summary and overview of individual topics and issues in Christian theology. For quick reference and ease in studying, the works are written in a question and answer format. The questions follow a logical progression so that those reading straight through a work will receive a greater appreciation for the topic and the issues involved. The volumes are thorough, though not exhaustive, and can be used as a set or as single volume studies. Each volume is fully documented and contains a recommended reading list for those who want to pursue the subject in greater detail.

The study of theology and the many issues within Christianity is an exciting and rewarding endeavor. For two thousand years, Christians have proclaimed the gospel of Jesus Christ and sought to accurately define and defend the doctrines of their faith as recorded in the Bible. In 2 Timothy 2:15, Christians are exhorted: "Be diligent to present yourself approved to God as a workman who does not need to be ashamed, accurately handling the word of truth." The goal of these books is to help you in your diligence and accuracy as you study God's Word and its influence in history and thought through the centuries.

Introduction

The study of prophecy and its puzzling pieces is an endeavor that is detailed and complex, but not beyond comprehension or resolution. It is open to error, misinterpretation, and confusion. However, such possibilities should not cause any Christian to shy away from either the study of prophecy or engagement in honest and irenic discussions about it. If you will spend the time studying Bible prophecy, the rewards will be great and the satisfaction will remain with you as you grow in your knowledge and love of our Lord Jesus Christ and His Word.

There are hundreds of questions that can be asked regarding the verses of prophecy found in the Bible and the events they predict. Like a jigsaw puzzle with hundreds of pieces, so too is Bible prophecy. Our intent in the following pages is to provide what is, essentially, the borders of the prophetic jigsaw puzzle, so that you will be able to continue your study of prophecy within a framework.

The theological perspective presented throughout the series is that of premillennialism and pretribulationism. We recognize that this is not the only position embraced by evangelical Christians, but we believe that it is the most widely held and prominent perspective. It is also our conviction that premillennialism, and specifically pretribulationism, *best* explains the prophetic plan of God as revealed in the Bible. We have placed a list of recommended readings at the end of the book to help guide readers who want to pursue the subject further.

PART 1

What Is Bible Prophecy?

1. How much prophecy is in the Bible?

Prophecy permeates the pages of Scripture. "The number of prophecies in the Bible is so large," declares Old Testament scholar Dr. Walter Kaiser, "and their distribution so evenly spread through both Testaments and all types of literary forms that the interpreter is alerted to the fact that he or she is dealing with a major component of the Bible."[1] Dr. Kaiser reports that the late Dr. J. Barton Payne calculated that 27 percent of the Bible deals with prophecy. Only Ruth and Song of Solomon in the Old Testament, and the short Epistles of Philemon and 3 John in the New Testament have no prophetic portions at all. According to Dr. Kaiser, "The highest percentages of predictive material are found in the small books of Zephaniah (89 percent), Obadiah (81 percent), and Nahum (74 percent). In the New Testament, the honors go to Revelation (63 percent), Hebrews (45 percent), and 2 Peter (41 percent)."[2] In the New Testament, as many as one out of twelve verses deal with the second coming of Jesus Christ. In the Epistles, the second coming is found in one out of ten verses. Such preoccupation by God in His Word with the subject of prophecy is not something that should be neglected or dismissed. How a person views prophetic events, including the second coming, greatly affects his or her view of present-day Christian living and spirituality.

2. How does the Bible use terms like "end times"?

There are a number of different expressions that appear in the Bible to speak of the end times. Sometimes people read in the Bible about the "last days," "end times," etc., and tend to think that all of these phrases all of the time refer to the same thing. This is not the case. Just as in our own lives, there are many endings. There is the end of the workday, the end of the day according to the clock, the end of the week, the end of the month, and the end of the year. Just because the word "end" is used does not mean that it always refers to the same time. The word "end" is restricted and precisely defined when it is modified by the prepositional phrase "of the day," "of the week," "of the year," etc. So it is in the Bible, that the term "end times" may refer to the end of the current church age or it may refer to the end of other times.

The Bible teaches that this present age will end with the rapture, followed by the tribulation which will end with the second coming of Messiah to the earth. Thus, we must distinguish between the "last days" of the present age, the church age, and the "last days" of Israel's future tribulation. Note the following chart that classifies and distinguishes between passages referring to the end of the church age and the "last days" for Israel.

Biblical Use of Last Days

Israel	Church
"latter days"—Deuteronomy 4:30; 31:29; Jeremiah 30:24; 48:47; Daniel 2:28; 10:14	"later times"—1 Timothy 4:1
"last days"—Isaiah 2:2; Jeremiah 23:20; 49:39; Ezekiel 38:16; Micah 4:1; Acts 2:17	"last days"—2 Timothy 3:1; Hebrews 1:2; James 5:3; 2 Peter 3:3
"last day"—John 6:39, 40, 44, 54; 11:24; 12:48	"last times"—1 Peter 1:20; Jude 18
"latter years"—Ezekiel 38:8	"last time"—1 Peter 1:5; 1 John 2:18

The Bible clearly speaks of a last day or end time, but it does not always refer to the same period of time with that phrase. The contextual referent enables the reader to know whether the Bible is speaking of the last days relating to Israel or the end times in reference to the church.

3. How should Bible prophecy be interpreted?

Words matter. They have meanings and they are used in a variety of ways in any and every language. Part of the process of what is known as hermeneutics, or the interpreting of literary texts, is understanding the framework within which any interpretation is made. Consistent literal interpretation is essential to properly understanding what God is saying in the Bible. Yet some people believe that consistent literal interpretation is either impossible or impractical. One critic believes it to be a "presumption" that "is unreasonable" and "an impossible ideal."[3] In spite of false characterization, what do we mean by consistent literal interpretation?

The dictionary defines *literal* as "belonging to letters." Further, it says literal interpretation involves an approach "based on the actual words in their ordinary meaning, . . . not going beyond the facts."[4] Literal interpretation is something that is very easily understood and done: "Literal interpretation of the Bible simply means to explain the original sense of the Bible according to the normal and customary usages of its language."[5] How is this done? It can only be accomplished through an interpretation of the written text, that includes consideration of the grammatical (according to the rules of the grammar of the original languages), historical (consistent with the historical setting of the passage), and contextual (in accord with its literary context) aspects of interpretation.

Grammatical Interpretation

The grammatical aspect of literal interpretation considers the impact that grammar has on a passage. This means that any person studying the text should correctly analyze the grammatical relationships that words, phrases, and sentences have with one another. Biblical scholar Dr. Roy Zuck writes:

> When we speak of interpreting the Bible grammatically, we are referring to the process of seeking to determine its meaning by ascertaining four things: (a) the meaning of words (lexicology), (b) the form of words (morphology), (c) the function of words (parts of speech), and (d) the relationships of words (syntax).[6]

Dr. Zuck gives further amplification of the four areas noted previously:

> In the meaning of words (lexicology), we are concerned with (a) etymology—how words are derived and developed, (b) usage—how words are used by the same and other authors, (c) synonyms and antonyms—how similar and opposite words are used, and (d) context—how words are used in various contexts.
>
> In discussing the form of words (morphology) we are looking at how words are structured and how that affects their meaning. For example the word *eat* means something different from *ate*, though the same letters are used. The word *part* changes meaning when the letter *s* is added to it to make the word *parts*. The function of words (parts of speech) considers what the various forms do. These include attention to subjects, verbs, objects, nouns, and others, as will be discussed later. The relationships of words (syntax) are the way words are related or put together to form phrases, clauses, and sentences.[7]

The grammatical aspect of literal interpretation lets the reader know that any interpretation conflicting with grammar is invalid.

Historical Interpretation

Proper interpretation of the Bible means that the historical context must be taken into account. This aspect means that one must consider the historical setting and circumstances in which the books of the Bible were written. Dr. Paul Tan explains:

> The proper concept of the historical in Bible interpretation is to view the Scriptures as written during given ages and cultures. Applications may then be drawn which are relevant to our times. For instance, the subject of meat offered to idols can only be interpreted from the historical and cultural setting of New Testament times. Principles to be drawn are relevant to us today.[8]

Understanding the cultural and historical background for a passage is crucial to accurate interpretation.

Contextual Interpretation

Any passage that is taken out of context is a pretext and leads to error in interpretation. Yet, one of the most common mistakes made by those who are found to have misinterpreted a passage in the Bible is that of taking a verse out of its divinely ordered context. Even though a sentence may be taken from the Bible, it is not the Word of God if it is placed into a context that changes the meaning from that which God intended in its original context. Dr. Zuck writes:

> The context in which a given Scripture passage is written influences how that passage is to be understood. Context includes several things:
> - the verse(s) immediately before and after a passage
> - the paragraph and book in which the verses occur
> - the dispensation in which it was written
> - the message of the entire Bible

- the historical-cultural environment of that time when it was written.[9]

A widely used example of a verse taken out of context is 2 Chronicles 7:14: "My people who are called by My name humble themselves and pray . . . ." Frequently this verse is quoted as an explanation of social and moral decline in the United States. Because "My people" are addressed, it is said that the success of a nation is dependent upon the obedience of Christians to the Lord. Thus, God blesses or curses a nation in accordance with Christian obedience. Then 2 Chronicles 7:14 is cited as a formula for national restoration because the passage says to "humble themselves and pray and seek My face and turn from their wicked ways, then I will hear from heaven, will forgive their sin and will heal their land."

We believe that this is an illustration of a passage taken out of context because of the following contextual factors:

- "My people" are said in 2 Chronicles 6:24 to be "Israel" as is also indicated by the flow of the historical context.
- Solomon is preparing to dedicate the recently completed Temple and 7:14 is God's renewal of the Mosaic covenant under which Israel and only Israel operates.

Since this passage involves Israel and not the church, it is improper to speculatively relate it to present-day Christianity in the United States or elsewhere. Proper contextual interpretation allows for the general observation that God delights in a humble and obedient people, but obedience and prayer should be offered according to His plan for the church.

Figures of Speech

Literal interpretation recognizes that a word or phrase can be used either plainly (denotative) or figuratively (connotative). As in our own conversations today, the Bible may use plain speech, such as "He died yesterday" (denotative use of language). Or the same thing may be said in a more colorful way, "He kicked the bucket yesterday" (connotative use of language). An important point to be noted is that even though we may use a figure of speech to refer to someone's death, we are using that figure to refer to an event that literally happened. Some interpreters mistakenly think that because a figure of speech may be used to describe an event (i.e., Jonah's experience in the belly of the great fish in Jonah 2), the event was not literal. However, such is not the case. A "golden rule of interpretation" has been developed to help us discern whether or not usage of a figure of speech was intended by an author: When the plain sense of Scripture makes common sense, seek no other sense; therefore, take every word at its primary, ordinary, usual, literal meaning unless the facts of the immediate context, studied in the light of related passages and axiomatic and fundamental truths, indicate clearly otherwise.[10]

For example, literalists understand that a figure of speech is employed by Isaiah teaching that the Adamic curse upon nature (Gen. 3:8–24) will be reversed in the millennium when he says, "And all the trees of the field will clap their hands" (Isa. 55:12). This figure is discerned by specific factors in the context in which it was written, all dealing with the removal of the curse upon nature at this future time. Even though figurative language is employed, it will literally happen in the course of human history.

Literal versus Literal

Dr. Elliott Johnson, a longtime professor of Bible and hermeneutics, has noted that much of the confusion over literal interpretation can be removed when one properly understands the two primary ways the term literal interpretation has been used throughout church history: "(1) the clear, plain sense of a word or phrase as over against a figurative use, and (2) a system that views the text as providing the basis of the true interpretation."[11] Thus, literalists, by and large have used the term *literal* to refer to their system of interpretation (the consistent use of the grammatical-historical system; Johnson's second), and once inside that system, *literal* refers to whether or not a specific word or phrase is used in its context in a figurative or literal sense (Johnson's first definition).

Johnson's second use of literal (i.e., systematic literalism) is simply the grammatical-historical system consistently used. The grammatical-historical system was revived by the Protestant Reformers in the sixteenth century. It was set against the spiritual (spiritualized) or "deeper" meaning of the text that was a common approach during the Middle Ages. The literal meaning was used simply as a springboard to a deeper ("spiritual") meaning, which was viewed as more desirable. A classic spiritualized interpretation would for example, see the four rivers of Genesis 2—the Pishon, Havilah, Tigris and Euphrates—as representing the human body, soul, spirit and mind. Coming from such a system, the Reformers saw the need to get back to the literal or textual meaning of the Bible.

The system of literal interpretation is the grammatical-historical or textual approach to interpretation. Use of literalism in this sense could be called "macroliteralism." Within macroliteralism, the consistent use of the grammatical-historical system yields the interpretative conclusion, for example, that *Israel* always and only refers to national Israel. The church will not be substituted for Israel if the grammatical-historical system of interpretation is consistently used because there are no indicators in the text of Scripture that such is the case. Therefore, one must bring an idea from outside the text by saying that the passage really means something that it does not actually say. This kind of replacement approach is a mild form of spiritualized, or allegorical, interpretation. So it is true to speak of those who replace *Israel* with *the church* as not taking the Bible literally and spiritualizing the text, since such a belief is contrary to a macroliteral interpretation.

Consistent literal interpreters, within the framework of the grammatical-historical system, do discuss whether or not a word, phrase, or the literary genre of a biblical book is a figure of speech (connotative) or is to be taken literally/plainly (denotative). There is discussion among literalists as to whether or not a given word or phrase is being used as a figure of speech, based on the context of a given passage. Some passages are quite naturally clearer than others and a consensus among interpreters develops, whereas other passages may find literal interpreters divided as to whether or not they should be taken as a figure of speech. However, this is more a problem of application than of method.

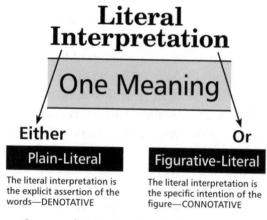

Courtesy of Earl Radmacher. Used by permission.

God's Word is to be understood through literal interpretation. This is very significant in the interpretation of prophetic passages and the study of eschatology (the doctrine of the last things). It is also an important foundation stone supporting the doctrine of the pretribulational rapture, a view of the future to which we as authors adhere (and which is discussed in further detail in the coming pages). When the Bible is consistently interpreted literally, from Genesis to Revelation, the pretribulational position is hard to avoid.

4. What is premillennialism?

Premillennialism is one of the three major views of Bible prophecy (the others are amillennialism and postmillennialism). Premillennialism teaches that the second coming of Jesus Christ to the earth (known also as the second advent), will occur before the establishment of the thousand-year reign of Jesus Christ from Jerusalem described in Revelation 20:1–7. This reign is known as the millennium.

The English theological term *premillennialism* comes from the Latin elements *pre* (before), *mille* (thousand), and *annus* (year). Premillennialism means that Jesus Christ will return to the earth "before the thousand years."

There are hundreds of millennium references in the Old Testament that speak of the time of Israel's end-time restoration to the land in blessing. However, it is not until John receives his revelation on the island of Patmos at the end of the New Testament era that the length of the Messiah's earthly reign is specified.

In the early church, premillennialism was called *chiliasm* (from the Greek term *chilioi* meaning "one thousand" used six times in Revelation 20:2–7). Theologian Dr. Charles Ryrie cites essential features of premillennial view of Christ's reign as follows: "Its duration will be 1,000 years; its location will be on this earth; its government will be theocratic with the personal presence of Christ reigning as King; and it will fulfill all the yet-unfulfilled promises about the earthly kingdom."[12]

Dispensational premillennialism (the majority premillennial view) holds that there will be a future, literal thousand year reign of Jesus Christ upon the earth following the events of the rapture, tribulation, and second coming.

Dispensational premillennialists hold that Israel and the church are two separate and distinct entities throughout all of history, including the millennium. Covenant premillennialists hold that in the Old and New Testament eras, Israel and the church were the same, but in the millennium they will be separate.

There are several forms of premillennialism that differ as to how the rapture relates to the tribulation but all teach that the millennium is one thousand literal years and follows Christ's second advent.

Premillennialism, or chiliasm as it was known in the early church, was the earliest of the three millennial systems to arise. Church historian Philip Schaff explains:

> The most striking point in the eschatology of the ante-Nicene Age is the prominent chiliasm, or millenarianism, that is the belief of a visible reign of Christ in glory on earth with the risen saints for a thousand years, before the general resurrection and judgment. It was indeed not the doctrine of the church embodied in any creed or form of devotion, but a widely current opinion of distinguished teachers.[13]

Premillennialism fell out of favor during the Middle Ages, but was revived by the Puritans in the seventeenth century. It is the viewpoint of a majority of those who are conservative in their approach to biblical interpretation.

Premillennialism is contrasted with the postmillennial teaching that Christ will return after reigning spiritually through the church from His throne in heaven for a long period of time during the current age. Premillennialism is also contrasted with the amillennial view that also advocates a present, but pessimistic, spiritual reign of Christ. Biblical premillennialism is a necessary foundation for pretribulationism since it is impossible for either postmillennialism or amillennialism to support pretribulationism.

Premillennialism

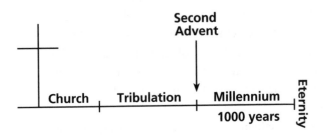

Premillennialism is simply the result of interpreting the whole Bible, Genesis to Revelation, in the most natural and normative way—literally. Many of the critics of premillennialism admit that if the literal approach is applied consistently to the whole of Scripture, then premillennialism is the natural result. If the Old Testament promises are ever going to be fulfilled literally for Israel as a nation, then they are yet in the future. This is also supportive of premillennialism. Premillennialism also provides a satisfactory and victorious end to history in time as humanity through Christ satisfactorily fulfills the creation mandate to rule over the world.

5. What is amillennialism?

Amillennialism is the view or system of eschatology (doctrine of the last things) that holds that there is no literal earthly millennium (thousand-year reign of Jesus Christ on the earth). Amillennialists believe that the millennium is spiritual. While all versions of amillennialism unite around their belief in no earthly millennium, they sometimes differ as to the exact nature and time of the millennium. While all believe that the millennium is spiritual and thus not earthly, some believe that the spiritual kingdom is present during the current era of the church. Some amillennialists believe that the present spiritual reign of God's kingdom consists of the influence that the church exerts through its many worldwide ministries.

Another form teaches that the millennium is composed of the reign of all dead Christians in heaven. Yet another kind believes that the millennium is equal to the eternal state that will commence at the second coming of Jesus Christ to the earth (known also as the second advent). In this view, the new heavens and new earth equals the millennium.

Amillennialism teaches that from the ascension of Christ in the first century until His second coming (no rapture) both good and evil will increase in the world as God's kingdom parallels Satan's kingdom. When Jesus Christ returns the end of the world will occur with a general resurrection and general judgment of all people. It is essentially a spiritualization of the kingdom prophecies.

Amillennialism was not present in the earliest era of the church. (At least there is no positive record of its existence.) It appears to have developed as a result first of opposition to premillennial literalism, and then evolved into a formal system. Amillennialism came to dominate the church when the great church father and theologian Augustine (354–430) abandoned premillennialism for amillennialism. It would probably be safe to say that amillennialism has been the most widely held view for much of the church's history, including most of the Protestant Reformers of the sixteenth century. Dr. Ryrie writes of amillennialism:

> One of the popular reasons for preferring amillennialism over premillennialism contrasts the premillennial concept of fulfillment in an earthly kingdom (usually the adjective *carnal* is placed with this phrase) with the amillennial concept of fulfillment of Old Testament prophecies in the church in this age (and usually the adjective *spiritual* is put with this phrase). Thus the system which emphasizes the spiritual church rather than the carnal kingdom is to be preferred. When I hear or read this argument, I want to ask, Since when is the church only spiritual and the kingdom only carnal? The church (look around) has carnal

people in it, and the kingdom will have many spiritual facets to it. Spiritual and carnal characterize both the church and the future kingdom.[14]

Always, of course, the conclusive evidence for the truth of a doctrine is not its historical legacy, but rather, its exegetical accuracy.

Amillennialism

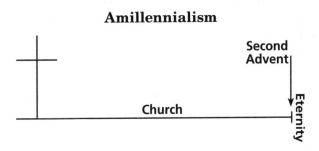

6. What is postmillennialism?

Postmillennialism is the view or system of eschatology (doctrine of the last things) teaching that the current age is the millennium, which is not necessarily a thousand years. Postmillennialists believe that the kingdom of Jesus Christ will gradually be extended though the preaching of the gospel; the eventual conversion of a majority of people (not necessarily all people); and the progressive growth of righteousness, prosperity, and development in every sphere of life as this growing majority of Christians struggle to subdue the world for Christ. Only after Christianity has dominated the world for a long time will Jesus Christ then return. After the church's glorious reign of victory (like amillennialism), there will be a general resurrection, destruction of the present creation, and entry into the eternal state. Postmillennialism differs from premillennialism and amillennialism in that postmillennialists are optimistic that this victory will be realized without the need for a cataclysmic return of Christ to impose righteousness. Instead, they believe that it will result from the faithful application of the present process.

Postmillennialism did not develop into a distinct system of eschatology until after the Reformation. Prior to that time, various elements developed that later were included in the theological mix of modern postmillennialism. Postmillennialism was the last major millennial position to develop.

Dr. John Walvoord, probably the greatest scholar and teacher of prophecy in the twentieth century, noted that there are two principle types of postmillennialism:

> Stemming from [Daniel] Whitby [1638–1726], these groups provided two types of postmillennialism which have persisted to the twentieth century: (1) a Biblical type . . . finding its material in the Scriptures and its power in God; (2) the evolutionary or liberal theological type which bases its proof on confidence in man to achieve progress through natural means. These two widely separated systems of belief have one thing in common, the idea of ultimate progress and solution of present difficulties.[15]

Postmillennialism was the dominant view of the millennium in the United States during much of the nineteenth century, but virtually became extinct up until the 1960s. The last several decades have witnessed an upsurge in postmillennialism in some conservative arenas through the Christian Reconstruction movement. (Various lists have been made of the key beliefs of the Reconstructionists, but those beliefs most central to Reconstructionism are: [1] A belief in the sovereignty of God; [2] Postmillennialism; [3] The application of the judicial laws of Moses in modern society; [4] Presuppositional apologetics; [5] The "covenant" concept as the key to understanding the Bible and history and the basis of Christian living. Christian Reconstructionists propose to institute a theocratic—that is, God-ruled—government in America, and they are gaining support in some elements of the evangelical community.) [16]

Postmillennialism

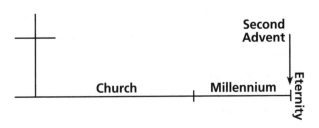

7. What is preterism?

Preterism is a term that is used to explain how some interpret Revelation chapters 4–19 in relation to the present. Preterism comes from a Latin word meaning "past" or "gone by." In its fullest expression, preterism teaches that Jesus Christ has already returned to the earth and that we are now living in the kingdom age.[17] Although preterists often focus on the Olivet Discourse, especially Matthew 24, the system was originally developed as an interpretive approach to Revelation.

The preterist approach to Revelation holds that the Apostle John wrote the book of Revelation around A.D. 65, since it was a prophecy about the impending destruction of Jerusalem that occurred in A.D. 70 through the Roman conquest. Preterists believe that the Roman emperor Nero (A.D. 37–68) was the Beast of Revelation or the Antichrist and that the tribulation period began three and a half years before August of A.D. 70, when Rome conquered Jerusalem. Thus, preterists believe Christ's return in Revelation 19 occurred non-bodily through the attacking Roman army.

There are three types of preterism. The first kind that appeared in the seventeenth century is called "mild" preterism. This view holds that the book of Revelation is about God defeating His two ancient enemies: first, the Jews in chapters 6–11, and secondly, the Romans in chapters 12–19. Thus, early preterism was less dependent on the

A.D. 70 event. We are not aware of anyone living today who holds this "mild" version of preterism.

The second type of preterism is often known as "partial" preterism. This view was developed originally by German liberals between 1785 and 1835 as a naturalistic way to interpret Revelation. Partial preterists see Revelation 6–19 as referring only to the destruction of Jerusalem and the Temple in A.D. 70. This is the version that is most popular today and has advocates such as R. C. Sproul, Kenneth Gentry, Gary DeMar, Hank Hanegraaff, and David Chilton.

The third type of preterism is known as "full" or "consistent" preterism. This view appears to have arisen sometime in the mid-1800s in the English-speaking world. Full preterism teaches that the entire book of Revelation was fulfilled through the A.D. 70 events. Full preterists believe that all biblical prophecy has been fulfilled and the second coming happened in the first century. This is clearly a heretical view since it denies a future second coming and accompanying resurrection. Most full preterists believe that we are now in the new heavens and new earth (i.e., "transmillennialism") and that the earth and the universe will continue as it is today for all eternity. Advocates of this view today include Max King and John Bray.

Arguments for preterism are usually grounded in preterists' interpretation of the teachings of Jesus in the Olivet Discourse (Matthew 24) and in their interpretation of the date of the writing of the book of Revelation. Let's look briefly at them.

Preterism and the Olivet Discourse

All preterists use Matthew 24:34 as a proof-text for their position.[18] In the passage Jesus declares: "Truly I say to you, this generation will not pass away until all these things take place." Preterists contend that Matthew 24:34 is saying that "this generation" must refer to Christ's contemporaries and therefore, the prophesied events by Christ of verses 4–31 had to occur within 40 years of Christ's departure from the earth. They argue that the events of verses 4–31 describe the Roman conquest of Jerusalem that was completed in August of A.D. 70, making Matthew 24:34 a past rather than a future prophecy.

However, based upon the grammar of the passage, "this generation" is modified by the phrase "all these things." In context, "all these things" refers to the events prophesied by Jesus in verses 4–31. Therefore, the key to understanding when "all these things" will take place is to discern whether they have already been fulfilled in the past or will they occur in the future. Since "all these things" will be fulfilled in the future, then "this generation" refers to the generation that will be alive to see the events of the seven-year tribulation period that are described in verses 4–31. Events like the arrival of false christs, the global preaching of the gospel, the abomination of desolation, global judgments, the second advent of Jesus, and the gathering of Jewish believers in order to bring them to Israel did not happen in the past, but await future fulfillment. The generation that sees all the prophesied events of the tribulation is the generation of which Christ refers in Matthew 24:34.

Preterism and the Date of the Book of Revelation

Preterists teach that the book of Revelation was written around A.D. 65 because the book was a prophecy about things that would happen between March A.D. 67 and August A.D. 70.[19] Since Revelation is a prophecy about the future, a preterist must hold to a date prior to the beginning of the fulfillment of the prophecies. Thus, they argue that Revelation was written during the reign of Nero in A.D. 65. This means that if Revelation was written under the reign of the emperor Domitian (A.D. 51–96), around A.D. 95, it renders the preterist viewpoint an impossibility.

The evidence for the A.D. 95 date of Revelation is overwhelming and has been the traditional view of the church since the second century. Irenaeus (second century to ca. 202)—a disciple of Polycarp (ca. A.D. 69–ca. 155) who was discipled by the Apostle John, author of Revelation—wrote in *Against Heresies* (about

A.D. 180) the following: "But if it had been necessary to announce his name plainly at the present time, it would have been spoken by him who saw the apocalypse. For it was not seen long ago, but almost in our own time, at the end of the reign of Domitian."[20] This is an explicit statement about when Revelation was written, which would be about A.D. 95. All the early church fathers held this view, as have almost all scholars down through church history, except, primarily those who hold the preterist view.

Polycarp was the bishop of the church of Smyrna, one of the seven churches to which Revelation is addressed in Revelation 2–3. He was alive when Revelation was written. Polycarp writes that the church of Smyrna did not even exist during the ministry of Paul.[21] Paul's ministry came to an end around A.D. 64. Thus, one of the seven churches of Revelation was not even in existence in A.D. 65.

Another of the churches of Revelation, the church of Laodicea, was devastated by an earthquake in either A.D. 60 or 61. It took about thirty years for the city to be rebuilt. Revelation 3:17 says, "Because you say, 'I am rich, and have become wealthy, and have need of nothing,'" would make no sense in A.D. 65, but does fit the condition of the city and the church in A.D. 95.

Nero's persecution was local, only in Rome. On the other hand, Domitian proclaimed the first Empire-wide persecution. Nero killed Christians such as Peter and Paul, however, Domitian was known to have exiled Christians, like a female relative named Domitilla exiled to an island named Pontia in A.D. 95 or 98 for being a Christian.[22] If Revelation were written in A.D. 65, why would Nero have killed Peter and Paul, yet exiled John to a remote island?

It is very unwise to construct one's entire views of prophecy on the foundation of the early date of Revelation, which at the very best is strongly disputed. Why would anyone adopt a view that is totally dependent on such a shaky foundation—especially when the A.D. 95 date is the view of the vast majority of scholars past and present?[23]

Preterism and the Text of Revelation

Preterists teach that the terms "soon" (Rev. 1:1) and "near" (Rev. 1:3) mean that the prophecies of the book had to occur within about a forty-year period. Preterists wrongly classify "soon" as an adverb of time. However, Greek grammar experts specifically cite "soon" as an adverb of manner, meaning that the focus of the word is on *how* something takes place, not *when*. Thus, it means when something begins to take place, it will happen suddenly or quickly. The word *near* means "close at hand." Within the context of Revelation "near" has the meaning of an overhanging imminence that the end times are near; they are the next series of prophetic events that will unfold. Imminency describes an event possible any day, impossible no day, thus conveying the urgency of the message of Revelation.

The clear language of Revelation speaks of global and supernatural events, while preterists want to allegorize these texts into local and naturalistically explained events. Preterists teach that Revelation is about God divorcing His former wife Israel and taking the church as His new bride. In reality, Revelation is about God preserving the Jewish remnant (Rev. 12) and rescuing them from danger at the second coming (Rev. 19). It is about salvation, not judgment, for Israel! Revelation depicts how history will move from the problems of the garden in Genesis to the New Jerusalem at the end of Revelation. If preterism were true, there is no climax for history. The true meaning is that the prophecies of Revelation are yet to be fulfilled in the future.

Some Implications of Preterism

All doctrine has practical implications.[24] What are the practical implications of those who hold to the view that most—and in some cases all—Bible prophecy has already been fulfilled? First, false doctrine is taught. Something is advocated that the Bible does not teach. Preterism teaches that Christ returned in A.D. 70. Second, the true meaning of a misinterpreted text is not understood. Preterism either teaches no future second coming, or it shrinks to near extinction the truth of "the blessed hope" (Titus 2:13). Even if there were not practical implications, the doctrinal error is great. Preterism greatly distorts the culmination of God's plan for history.

If preterism is true—especially full preterism—then we are already at the end of history and don't really know specifically where history is headed. In fact, even partial preterist Kenneth Gentry says of Revelation 21–22:

> The new creation begins in the first century. . . . My understanding of this antithesis is that the new Jerusalem is replacing the old Jerusalem. The coming of the new Jerusalem down from heaven (chaps. 21–22) logically should follow soon upon the destruction of the old Jerusalem on the earth (Rev. 6–11; 14–19), rather than waiting thousands of years.[25]

Thus, Gentry believes that we are in some way in the new heavens and new earth of Revelation 21–22. If this is true, then we all must be living in the ghetto side of the New Jerusalem. Such a false teaching reminds one of the Hindu belief that says that current reality is "Maya"—a mere illusion—especially the current existence of evil.[26]

The logic of the preterist position leads one to delusional views of present reality. "The overwhelming majority of the eschatological events prophesied in the book of Revelation have already been fulfilled," declares preterist Gary North.[27] Since subjects relating to prophecy dominate virtually every page of the New Testament this would logically mean, for the preterist, that most of the New Testament does not refer directly to the church and Christians today. Since so much of the New Testament is written to tell Christians how to live between the two comings of Christ, it makes an enormous difference if one interprets Christ's coming as a past or future event. If preterism is true, then the New Testament refers to Christians who lived during the forty-year period between the death of Christ and the destruction of Jerusalem in A.D. 70. Therefore, virtually no part of the New Testament applies to Christians today according to preterist logic. There is no canon that applies directly to Christians during the church age.

Not only does Gentry believe that the great tribulation is a past event, he believes that current history is identified as the new heavens and new earth of Revelation 21–22 and 2 Peter 3:10–13.[28] This is a common preterist viewpoint. Talk about lowering expectations! Gentry provides four major reasons why "the new creation begins in the first century."[29] It stretches credulity to think of the implications of the details of such a conclusion. If we are currently living in any way in the new heavens and new earth then this means the following:

- The one thousand years and the new heavens and earth must be equated (cf. 20:1–9 with 21–22)
- Satan has been removed from any more influence in history (20:10)
- There is no longer any sea (21:1)
- There is no longer any death, crying, or pain (21:4)
- All things have been made new (21:5)
- There is no longer any need for the sun or the moon (21:23)
- There is no longer any night (21:25)
- There is no longer any unclean, nor those practicing abomination and lying (21:27)
- There is no longer any curse (22:3)
- Believers are now able to see the Father's face (22:4)
- There is no longer any sun (22:5)

If Revelation 21–22 is a description of the state in which we are now living then it also renders most of the New Testament obsolete and impractical since it relates to believers and how they should live between Christ's two comings. The logic of the preterist position would lead to this conclusion, even though many preterists do not think this way in practice. They don't, but they should!

Jesus said in the great commission of Matthew 28:20, "and lo, I am with you always, even to the end of the age." Thus, it follows from preterist logic, that the age, which Christ spoke of in His great commission, culminated in A.D. 70. The practical implication would be that since "the end of the age" concluded in A.D. 70, Christ is no longer with us as we carry out His commission.

Preterism and the Sufferings of This Present Time

The new heavens and new earth are to be a time of peace and rest for God's people. The era preceding this time of peace will be one of suffering and struggle. But if the preterist interpretation is correct, then the instruction of the New Testament Epistles on the issue of suffering only directly applied to Christians until A.D. 70, because we would now be in the time of peace, not "the sufferings of this present time" spoken of by Paul (Rom. 8:18).

Endurance of unjust suffering is a major theme in the Epistles. In fact, the New Testament portrays it as one of the major ingredients that God brings into our lives to produce Christlike character (Heb. 12:1–17). Peter notes, "For this [unjust suffering] finds favor, if for the sake of conscience toward God a person bears up under sorrows when suffering unjustly. . . . But if when you do what is right and suffer for it you patiently endure it, this finds favor with God" (1 Peter 2:19–20).

Revelation promises a future reward of corulership with Christ to believers who have remained faithful and loyal to Christ during this present age of humiliation (Rev. 3:21; see also 2:25–28). Revelation 3:21 not only promises future rule with Christ after this current age of humiliation, but it also makes a distinction between Christ's future kingdom and God the Father's current rule. "He who overcomes, I will grant to him to sit down with Me on My throne, as I also overcame and sat down with My Father on His throne." These passages do not make sense and certainly do not apply to today if we are in the new heavens and new earth of the preterists.

When Bible prophecy is taken literally it leads to a proper understanding of God's plan for history and the individual believer. Such an understanding provides a great hope, indeed a "blessed hope" that Christ's prophetic program for the church and Israel will yet provide some of the greatest moments of history. A futurist eschatology provides a fitting climax for history that began in a garden and concludes in a city—the New Jerusalem. Christ's church will be raptured before the tribulation so that our Lord can complete His plan for His ancient people Israel. The tribulation is a time in which God will rescue, not judge, the Jews so that "all Israel will be saved." The tribulation and much of Bible prophecy is not past; rather, it is future. If it is in the past, as preterism teaches, then we have no future.

8. Is the fulfillment of Bible prophecy best understood as being past, present, or future?

We believe the answer to this question is "future." Part of the foundation for a systematic understanding of the pretribulation rapture (in addition to literal interpretation, premillennialism, and distinguishing Israel from the church) is futurism. An important, but seemingly little-recognized aspect of proper interpretation of Bible prophecy is the role of timing. When will a prophecy be fulfilled in history? There are four possibilities. The four views are simple in the sense that they reflect the only four possibilities in relation to time—past, present, future, and timeless.

The *preterist* view (past) believes that most, if not all, prophecy has already been fulfilled, usually in relation to the destruction of Jerusalem in A.D. 70. The *historicist* view (present) sees much of the current church age as equal to the tribulation period. Thus, prophecy has been and will be fulfilled during the current church age. The *futurist* view (future) believes that virtually all prophetic events will not occur in the current church age, but will take place in the future tribulation, second coming, or millennium. The *idealist* view (timeless) does not believe either that the Bible indicates the timing of events or that we can determine their timing in advance. Idealists think that prophetic passages mainly teach great ideas or truths about God to be applied regardless of timing. In the chart below, the shading shows when each of these views understands that the fulfillment of prophecy occurs.

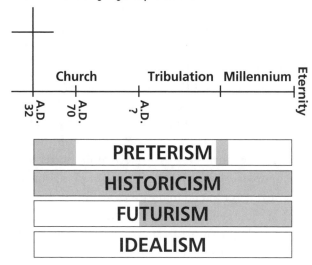

The Significance of Futurism

Of the four views noted above, the only one that logically and historically has supported the pretribulational position is futurism. Why? Because, the timing of the rapture relates to when the tribulation will occur in history. Preterism declares that the tribulation has already taken place. Historicism says that the tribulation started in the fourth century with events surrounding Constantine's Christianization of the Roman Empire and continues until the second coming. Idealism denies that there is a timing of events. Thus, only futurism, which sees the tribulation as a yet future event could even allow for a rapture before the beginning of that seven-year period. This does not mean, however, that all futurists are pretribulationists; they are not. *But to be a pretribulationist, one must be a futurist.*

Support for Futurism

A defense of futurism can be developed from the Bible by comparing and contrasting futurism with the other three views. For example, *futurism instead of preterism* can be shown by demonstrating from specific texts of Scripture that "coming" in the debated passages refer to a bodily return of Christ to the earth, not a mystical coming mediated through the Roman army. (Preterists normally use the texts in Matthew 24 and just declare that they can allow for a non-physical coming through the Roman army.)[30]

One area that supports *futurism instead of historicism* is demonstrated by the fact that numbers in the biblical text relating to days and years are to be taken literally. There is no biblical basis for days really meaning years. A major argument for *futurism instead of idealism* is the fact that numbers do count. In other words, why would God give hundreds of chronological and temporal statements in the Bible if He did not intend to indicate the time of events?

Let's look at some general support for the futurist approach. First and foremost, only the futurist can interpret the whole Bible literally and having done so harmonize those conclusions into a consistent theological system. Just as the people, places, and times were meant to be understood literally in Genesis 1–11, so are the texts that relate to the end times to be taken literally. Days mean days; years mean years; months mean months. Thus, the only way that the book of Revelation and other prophetic portions of the Bible make any sense is if they are taken literally, which means that they have not yet happened. Thus, they are future.

One third of the verses in the Bible are prophetic passages and the majority of those verses pertain to yet future prophetic events. Since a consistently literal approach to the whole Bible, including prophecy, is the proper way of understanding God's revelation to humanity, then the futurist approach is the correct way of looking at the timing of biblical prophecy. And, as stated before, only the futurist understanding of biblical prophecy can support the pretribulational rapture.

9. What is the relationship between Israel and the church in prophecy?

Much of the confusion about prophetic passages throughout church history has been a result of misunderstanding the relationship between Israel and the church. Misappropriating passages that refer to Israel rather than to the church has been a major interpretive pitfall for many Christians.

Israel and the church are distinct entities in Bible prophecy. "The New Testament consistently differentiates between Israel and the church," claims Dr. Arnold Fruchtenbaum.[31] Fruchtenbaum supports this conclusion through a powerful twofold argument in which he first demonstrates the biblical view of Israel and then shows that the church is viewed in the New Testament as a separate entity.

God has two peoples—Israel and the church. Belief that God's single plan for history includes the two peoples of Israel and the church does not imply that there are different ways of salvation. Christ's saving work is the only way of salvation for anyone, whether they are a member of Israel or the church.

Israel

Fruchtenbaum notes that "the term *Israel* is viewed theologically as referring to all descendants of Abraham, Isaac, and Jacob, also known as Jews, the Jewish people, Israelites, Hebrews, etc."[32] National election distinguishes Israel from those peoples who were not chosen (Gentiles). Four reasons for Israel's election can be presented: (1) They were "chosen on the basis of God's love . . . to be 'a kingdom of priests and a holy nation' (Exod. 19:6) . . . to represent the Gentile nations before God." (2) "God chose Israel to be the recipient of His revelation and to record it (Deut. 4:5–8; 6:6–9; Rom. 3:1–2)." (3) Israel "was to propagate the doctrine of the One God (Deut. 6:4)." (4) Israel "was to produce the Messiah (Rom. 9:5; Heb. 2:16–17; 7:13–14)."[33]

No biblically oriented Christian would deny these purposes

relating to Israel. The differences in understanding begin to emerge when we consider Israel in relation to the church. Fruchtenbaum notes:

> Some theologians insist that at some point the church receives the promises given to Israel and thus become the "New Israel" (known as replacement theology). Some believe the terms *church* and *Israel* are used virtually "interchangeably," most citing Galatians 6:16 and some Romans 9:6.[34]

It is this idea of replacement theology that creates much difficulty and dissention in accurately understanding prophecy. However, those commonly known as dispensationalists interpret the Bible literally and do not confuse or interchange the terms *Israel* and the *church*, since there is no basis in the text of any biblical passage for supporting such an approach.

Having noted important aspects of the biblical use of the term "Israel," we will now examine the nature of the church.

The Church

At least six reasons can be found from the Bible supporting the notion that the church is a distinct work in God's household from His people Israel.[35]

1. The church was born at Pentecost in A.D. 33 (Acts 2), whereas Israel had existed for many centuries. This is supported by Jesus' use of the future tense in Matthew 16:18, showing that the church did not yet exist in gospel history. The church born at Pentecost is called the "Body of Christ" (Col. 1:18), and entrance into the body is through "Spirit baptism" (1 Cor. 12:13), in which Jew and Gentile are united. It is evident that the church began on the Day of Pentecost since Acts 1:5 views Spirit baptism as future, while Acts 10 links it to the past, specifically to Pentecost.

2. Specific events in the ministry of Jesus were essential to the establishment of the church and it does not come into existence until these events have occurred. These events include the resurrection and ascension of Jesus to become head of the church (Eph. 1:20–23) and the coming of the Holy Spirit to provide spiritual gifts for the church to function (Eph. 4:7–11).

3. There is a mystery character of the church that was not revealed before the New Testament era. A mystery in the Bible is a hidden truth not revealed until the New Testament (Eph. 3:3–5, 9; Col. 1:26–27). Fruchtenbaum lists four defining characteristics of the church that are specifically described as a mystery and that distinguish the church from Israel: (1) the body concept wherein Jewish and Gentile believers are united into one body (Eph. 3:1–12); (2) the doctrine of Christ indwelling every believer (Col. 1:24–27, and see also Col. 2:10–19; 3:4); (3) the church being designated as the Bride of Christ (Eph. 5:22–32); and (4) the rapture (1 Cor. 15:50–58).[36]

4. According to Ephesians 2:15, there is the unique relationship between Jews and the Gentiles, called "one new man." During the present church age God is saving a remnant from the two previous entities (Israel and Gentiles) and combining them into a third new entity—the church. This unity of Jews and Gentiles into this new entity exists only in the church age—from Pentecost until the rapture—after which time God will restore Israel and complete her destiny (Acts 15:14–18). This division is reflected in 1 Corinthians 10:32: "Give no offense either to Jews or to Greeks or to the church of God."

5. The contrast between Galatians 6:16 (which speaks of "the Israel of God") and 1 Corinthians 10:18 (which speaks of "Israel after the flesh" KJV) shows a distinction between Jews believing in Jesus as Messiah and those who do not believe in Jesus as Messiah. The Galatians passage does not support the false claim of replacement theologians who claim that Israel is supplanted by the church.

Instead, the Bible teaches that a remnant of Israel is combined with elect Gentiles during this age to make up an entirely new entity that the New Testament calls "the church" (Eph. 2).

Replacement theology teaches that because Gentile believers are described as "Abraham's descendants" (Gal. 3:29), this is equivalent to saying that they are Israel. But this is clearly not the case. Paul's description of Gentile believers in Galatians 3:29 simply means that they participate in the spiritual (i.e., salvation) blessings that come through Israel (Rom. 15:27; 1 Cor. 9:11, 14). Gentiles are not partakers of Israel's physical, material, or national promises—only the spiritual blessings. Therefore, Israel's national promises are left intact awaiting a yet future fulfillment.

6. After Pentecost, throughout the book of Acts, Israel and the church exist simultaneously and as separate entities. The term *Israel* occurs twenty times and the term *ekklesia* (church) occurs nineteen times, and they are always distinct from each other. Thus, the replacement theologian has no actual biblical basis upon which to base the theological claim that Israel and the church have become one.

The Significance of the Distinction

If, when studying the Bible, Israel and the church are not distinguished then there is no basis for seeing a future for Israel or for the church as a new and unique people of God. If Israel and the church are merged into a single program, then the Old Testament promises for Israel will never be fulfilled and are usually seen by replacement theologians as being spiritually fulfilled by the church. The merging of Israel's destiny into the church's destiny not only makes into one what the Scriptures understand as two, but it also removes a need for future restoration of God's original elect people in order to literally fulfill His promise that Israel will one day "be the head and not the tail" (Deut. 28:13).

The more that Christians see a distinct plan for Israel and a distinct plan for the church, the more they realize that when the New

Testament speaks to the church it is describing a separate destiny and hope for it. The church becomes more distinct in the plan of God. Israel's future includes the seven-year tribulation, and then, shortly before Christ's return to Jerusalem in the event of the second coming, Israel will be converted to Jesus as the Messiah. For the church, its distinct hope for the future is the rapture, Christ's any-moment return.

A distinction between Israel and the church, as taught in the Bible, provides a basis of support for the pretribulational rapture. Those who merge the two programs cannot logically support the biblical arguments for pretribulationism.

10. What does the Bible teach about prophetic date-setting?

Jesus was quite emphatic in teaching about His return. In at least five passages (seven, if parallel passages are included) Jesus specifically warned the disciples and Christians against setting dates for the expected return of Christ. Yet, throughout church history there has been an amazing amount of date speculation.

Jesus emphasized prophecy and understanding it in His teachings. He did not avoid it or dismiss its relevance; He did just the opposite. He emphasized its importance in understanding His life and ministry. Yet, Jesus did explain that there are some aspects of the future that cannot be discerned with precision. His return is certain, but the precise moment is not. Jesus understood the human longing for knowledge of the future, but He did not permit His followers to succumb to soothsayer temptations:

- Matthew 24:36: "But of that day and hour no one knows, not even the angels of heaven, nor the Son, but the Father alone" (Mark 13:32 is an exact parallel).
- Matthew 24:42: "Therefore be on the alert, for you do not know which day your Lord is coming."
- Matthew 24:44: "For this reason you also must be ready; for

the Son of Man is coming at an hour when you do not think
He will."
- Matthew 25:13: "Be on the alert then, for you do not know the
  day nor the hour" (Mark 13:33–37 is a parallel passage).
- Acts 1:7: "He said to them, 'It is not for you to know times or
  epochs which the Father has fixed by His own authority.'"

These passages are absolute prohibitions against date setting.
Some students of prophecy have said that these verses teach that it
was impossible to know the date in the early church, but in the last
days some will come to know it. Others have said that the verses
teach that no one knows the day or the hour, except those who
are able to figure it out through some scheme. Both are absolutely
wrong! The date of Christ's coming is a matter of God's revelation
and He has chosen not to reveal it even to Christ in His humanity
during Jesus' first advent (Matthew 24:36). If the Father does not
reveal it to the Son in His humanity, why should any person believe
the Father would reveal it to him or her? Jesus' word on the issue of
setting dates is very clear—"no!"

The teaching of Jesus is reinforced elsewhere in the Scriptures
as well. In 1 Thessalonians 5:1–2, Paul writes, "Now as to the times
and the epochs, brethren, you have no need of anything to be written to you. For you yourselves know full well that the day of the
Lord will come just like a thief in the night." In this passage, Paul
reasserts the words of Jesus regarding the uncertainty of the time
of His return.

Some people believe that there are passages in the Bible that teach
that Christians will be able to know the date of Christ's return. We
will examine some of these passages to show how those who advo-
cate date setting have misused various verses in their attempts to
legitimize the practice. The Bible does not contain internal contra-
dictions. It is wrong to think that on the one hand Scripture says
"no man can know," but then on the other hand, that some people
will be able to figure it out.

The first passage that is sometimes cited is Luke 21:28: "But when these things begin to take place, straighten up and lift up your heads, because your redemption is drawing near." Some people have taught that this passage implies a license to date set. However, important contextual indicators are overlooked in such an argument. These indicators include the fact that the passage refers to Jewish believers during the future seven-year tribulation, who, right before the second coming of Christ, are told to *watch,* not date set, as they endure the final period of severe persecution. This does not relate to date setting during the current church age, since it speaks of events during the seven-year tribulation. Once the tribulation starts, then it will be possible to know the time of Christ's coming. However, this in no way relates to Christians today who are living during the church age rather than during the tribulation. The church age ends with the signless event of the rapture. Thus, there is no way to link, specifically, events of our own day with those of the tribulation for the purpose of setting a date. We are to be watching and waiting for our Lord's return at the rapture precisely because we cannot date-set.

A second passage sometimes cited is Hebrews 10:25: "but encouraging one another; and all the more as you see the day drawing near." Some teach that this implies that Christians are able to see or know that "the day" (the second coming) is drawing near. While some do interpret "the day" as a reference to the second coming, we think that the immediate context and the context of the book of Hebrews is one that is a warning to Jewish believers before the A.D. 70 destruction of Jerusalem and the temple. It is a warning not to return (i.e., apostatize) to Judaism, since the immediate future only contained wrath for those Jews who rejected Jesus as their Messiah. Therefore, "the day" is not a reference to the second coming but instead refers to Jerusalem's destruction by the Romans in A.D. 70. If this passage does refer to the second coming, once again there would be no basis for linking a specific factor on which to date the second coming. The general statement "as you see the day drawing near" does not mean that we will know specifically when He is coming any more than one watching the progress of a thunderstorm knows the precise moment when it will rain at his or her location.

A third passage that is sometimes called upon to set dates is 1 Thessalonians 5:4: "But you, brethren, are not in darkness, that the day should overtake you like a thief." It has been taught from this passage that Christians would have to know the timing of "the day" (i.e., "the day of the Lord," see 1 Thess. 5:2) in order to not be overtaken by it. But this date-setting interpretation attaches the wrong sense to Paul's teaching. Paul is saying that they will not be overtaken because they are prepared by virtue of the fact that they are believers. All Christians will be taken care of by the Lord (we believe through the pretribulational rapture), so that, unlike the unbeliever who will be unprepared and caught off guard, the believer will be prepared.

Sometimes Israel's feast cycle is looked to for date-setting schemes. The Bible teaches a cycle of seven feasts which Israel was to celebrate yearly. The seven feasts are: Passover, Unleavened Bread, Firstfruits, Feast of Weeks, Trumpets, Day of Atonement, and Tabernacles. The first four feasts are celebrated each spring, while the remaining three are commemorated in the fall.

A common interpretation by some evangelicals concludes that the feasts also are prophetic of the career of the Messiah. The spring cycle is said to have been fulfilled by Christ at His first coming, while the fall cycle will be fulfilled in the future through events surrounding the second coming. It seems that many of the more recent and popular date-setting schemes have implemented Israel's feast cycle in some way.

Up to this point, we have no problem with this scheme. However, we do have a problem with those who teach that the fifth feast (Trumpets) is a reference to the rapture. Rosh Hashanah (Hebrew for "Feast of Trumpets") is celebrated yearly on Tishri 1 according to the Hebrew calendar (this day usually falls in September according to our contemporary calendar), and it is argued that trumpets are related to the rapture (1 Cor. 15:52). Therefore, it is concluded, the rapture will occur on Tishri 1 as the fall cycle begins to be fulfilled. This view argues that if the year of the rapture can be determined, then we would know that it would occur in the fall of the year.

There is one major problem with this approach that disqualifies any use of it for date setting. Israel's feasts relate to Israel and Israel alone. It is true that the fulfillment of Israel's feasts relates to salvation for all humanity, but the precise fulfillment relates exclusively to national Israel and will be fulfilled through tribulation and millennial events when Israel is once again the direct instrument of God. The rapture is a new event related only to the church, and thus would not have been predicted through Old Testament revelation such as Israel's feasts. Therefore, any use of the feasts of Israel in an attempt to date set is invalid.

It should be clear that the church does not fulfill any of Israel's feasts, including the Day of Pentecost. The Feast of Pentecost was given for Israel. It just so happened that in the plan of God He scheduled the founding of the church to begin on that day, even though it is not a fulfillment by the church of the Feast of Pentecost. Any future fulfillment of the feasts will be fulfilled by Israel, not the church.

There is no harm in studying prophecy. In fact, we can't properly study the Bible and ignore prophecy, but we must not fall into a snare of setting dates. The Bible clearly teaches that God's Word is sufficient for everything needed to live a life pleasing unto Christ (2 Tim. 3:16–17; 2 Peter 1:3–4). This means that if something is not revealed for us in the Bible, it is not needed to accomplish God's plan for our lives. The date of Christ's return is not stated in the Bible, therefore, in spite of what some may say, knowing it is not important for living a godly life. The Lord told Israel "The secret things belong to the LORD our God, but the things revealed belong to us and to our sons forever, that we may observe all the words of this law" (Deut. 29:29). The date of Christ's coming has not been revealed, it is a secret belonging only to God.

Since the Bible prohibits date setting, what does it teach? Many of the same passages which prohibit date setting, at the same time instruct us what to do until the Lord returns. For example, Matthew 24:42 not only warns "for you do not know which day your Lord is coming," but also admonishes believers to "be on the alert." Matthew 24:44 tells believers to "be ready" because "the Son of Man is coming at an hour when you do not think He will." Also, Matthew 25:13 admonishes us to "be on the alert then, for you do not know the day nor the hour."

The alert to which believers are called is not to date setting, but one of looking for the Savior, since we do not know when He will return. We are to be alert, in contrast to unbelievers who are pictured as sleeping in regard to the things of God. We are to be alert for the purpose of godly living until the Lord does return because we are in the dark night of this current age, which requires an active alertness toward evil. While date setting is clearly prohibited in God's Word, we believe that it is valid to understand that God is setting the stage for His great end-time program. What does that mean? The rapture is a signless event, thus it is impossible to identify any signs that indicate its nearness. This is why all attempts to date the rapture have had to wrongly resort to applying to the church passages relating to God's plan for Israel.

Jesus Christ will return! It is our responsibility to be prepared for that return and to proclaim the salvation He offers, so others may also be prepared.

The hope for the Christian continues to be the return of the Lord Jesus Christ for His own in the rapture. Titus 2:13 admonishes Christians to be "looking for the blessed hope and the appearing of the glory of our great God and Savior, Christ Jesus." In the interim, we are to be faithful to Him, to proclaim the gospel of salvation to all who will listen, and to "do good to all people, and especially to those who are of the household of the faith" (Gal. 6:10). Regardless of what critics and scoffers may say, we are not pessimistic about the future. Rather, we are realistic and we are certain that regardless of tomorrow's headlines, our hope and our destiny is in Christ Jesus, the Final Victor.

Evangelical theologian Carl F. H. Henry astutely noted: "While the last days have replaced the past days, *the very last day, the very last hour,* remains future but draws ever closer. The last day is crowding and pressing upon the prophetic calendar."[37] His words are certainly true. Each day that we mark off the calendars we keep brings us closer to the coming of the Lord. Perhaps it will be today, perhaps tomorrow, perhaps a century from now. It will happen and it will happen according to God's predetermined plan. In the interim moments, we are to be faithful, ready, and waiting. We are not called to idleness, confusion, or complacency. As Dr. Henry noted four decades ago, "The barbarians are coming; the Lord Jesus Christ is coming. *Christians are here now; do they know whether they are coming or going?*"[38]

As Christians, we have a purpose and mission in this world. We are to be encouraged by prophecy, not distracted by it. We are not to set dates, for God has already done that and will not reveal them to us. We must focus on what He has revealed, rather than on what He has not. May our prayer be the same as the Apostle John's in Revelation 22:20, "Come, Lord Jesus."

PART 2

What Does the Bible Teach About the Rapture?

The doctrine of the pretribulational rapture offers Christians great hope for the future. The Bible never intends that doctrine and the spiritual life be separated. The study of prophecy and an understanding of the rapture provide us with both a knowledge of the Word of God and a daily hope for the return of Christ as we wait for Him and proclaim His gospel. It is not about escapism or avoiding the difficulties of this world. It is not about neglecting the concerns of life and the needs of others. Rather, it is a recognition that God has a prophetic plan and that Christians and the church are integral components in that plan. The rapture is not just wishful "pie in the sky in the by-and-by" thinking. Rather, it is vitally connected to Christian living in the "nasty here and now."

11. What is the rapture?

The pretribulational rapture teaches that prior to the seven-year tribulation, all Christians (both living and dead) will be caught up in the air to meet Christ and then taken to heaven. The teaching of the rapture is most clearly presented in 1 Thessalonians 4:13–18. In this passage Paul informs his readers that living Christians at the time of the rapture will be reunited with those who have died in Christ before them. In verse 17 the English phrase "caught up" translates the Greek word *harpazó*, which means "to seize upon with force" or "to snatch up." This word is used 14 times in the Greek New Testament in a variety of ways.

Sometimes the New Testament uses *harpazó* with the sense of "stealing," "carrying off," or "dragging away" (Matt. 12:29; John 10:12). It also can have the meaning of "to lead away forcibly" (John 6:15; 10:28, 29; Acts 23:10; Jude 23). However, for our purposes, a third usage is significant: God's Spirit carrying someone away. We see this usage four times (Acts 8:39; 2 Cor. 12:2, 4; 1 Thess. 4:17; Rev. 12:5).[1]

This latter usage is illustrated in Acts 8:39 where Philip, upon completion of the baptism of the Ethiopian eunuch, is "caught up" and divinely transported from the desert to the coastal town of Azotus. Similarly, the church will, in a moment of time, be taken from the earth to heaven.

Some critics have noted that the word "rapture" is never used in the Bible. While this is true of English versions, Latin translators of the Greek New Testament *did* use the Latin word *rapere*, which is the root of the English term *rapture*. Many contemporary theological terms have been derived from a Latin base. Throughout much of the history of the Western Church, Latin was the accepted language of theological discussion. As a result, many theological terms developed out of this language (i.e., Trinity). Our current term "rapture" is also such a term. As will be seen below, there are many terms used in the New Testament to refer to the rapture event. Thus, to claim that the rapture should be dismissed on the grounds of language is naively incorrect. The doctrine of the pretribulational rapture is an important biblical teaching not only because it provides insights into the future, but because it provides Christians with motivation for contemporary living.

12. What New Testament terms refer to the rapture?

The New Testament uses a variety of Greek terms to describe the multifaceted aspects of the rapture. (Emphasis has been added in the verses listed below.)

- *harpazó*—caught up; to seize upon with force; to snatch up
  "Then we who are alive and remain will *be caught up* together with them in the clouds to meet the Lord in the air, and so we shall always be with the Lord" (1 Thess. 4:17).
- *episunagógé*—gathering together; assembly
  "Now we request you, brethren, with regard to the coming of our Lord Jesus Christ and our *gathering together* to Him" (2 Thess. 2:1).
- *allassó*—to change; to transform; to exchange
  "Behold, I tell you a mystery; we will not all sleep, but we will all be *changed,* in a moment, in the twinkling of an eye, at the last trumpet; for the trumpet will sound, and the dead will be raised imperishable, and we will be *changed*" (1 Cor. 15:51–52).
- *paralambanó*—to take to; to receive to oneself
  "If I go and prepare a place for you, I will come again and *receive* you to Myself, that where I am, there you may be also" (John 14:3).
- *epiphaneia*—a manifestation; an appearance
  ". . . looking for the blessed hope and *the appearing* of the glory of our great God and Savior, Christ Jesus" (Titus 2:13).
- *rhuomai*—to draw to oneself; to rescue; to deliver
  ". . . and to wait for His Son from heaven, who He raised from the dead, that is Jesus, who *rescues* us from the wrath to come" (1 Thess. 1:10).
- *apokalupsis*—an uncovering; laying bare; a revealing, revelation
  "Therefore, prepare your minds for action, keep sober in spirit, fix your hope completely on the grace to be brought to you at *the revelation* of Jesus Christ" (1 Peter 1:13).

- *parousia*—a being present, presence; a coming; an arrival
  "Therefore be patient, brethren, until *the coming* of the Lord. The farmer waits for the precious produce of the soil, being patient about it, until it gets the early and late rains. You too be patient; strengthen your hearts, for *the coming* of the Lord is near" (James 5:7–8).

Not every use of these words in the New Testament is a rapture reference. The context determines its meaning. A review of these terms teaches that the rapture will be an event initiated by Christ in which He comes in the clouds and appears to Christians. His revelation will result in drawing, gathering, catching up, and receiving to Himself those same believers. During this event, Christians of all time will be transformed; the living will be translated apart from death, while those asleep in Christ will be resurrected. All these will then accompany the Son to the Father's heavenly house that He has prepared for them.

13. When does the rapture take place in relation to the tribulation?

There are five major views within premillennialism concerning the timing of the rapture in relation to the seven-year tribulation:

- *Pretribulationism*. This view teaches that all Christians will be taken in the rapture which will occur before the tribulation.

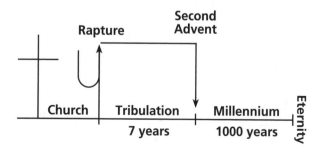

- *Partial rapture.* This view teaches that the rapture occurs before the tribulation, but only "spiritual" Christians will be taken, while other Christians will remain through the tribulation.

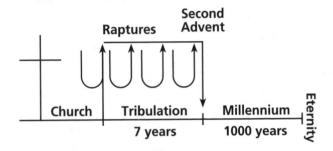

- *Midtribulationism.* This view teaches that all Christian will be taken in the rapture in the middle of the tribulation (after the first 3½ years).

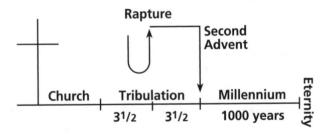

- *Pre-Wrath Rapture.* This view teaches that all Christians will be taken in the rapture approximately three-fourths of the way through the tribulation.

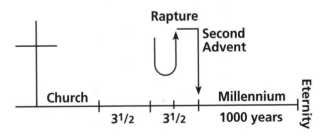

- *Posttribulationism.* This view teaches that all Christians will be raptured at the end of the tribulation.

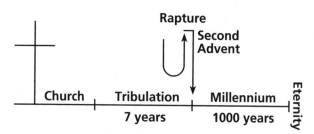

There are many arguments for and against each of the views listed above. However, the purpose of this book is to set forth a positive presentation of pretribulationism.

14. What is imminency and why is it significant for the rapture?

Imminency is the New Testament teaching that Jesus Christ could return and rapture the church at any moment, without prior signs or warning. It is such a powerful argument for pretribulationism that it is one of the most fiercely attacked doctrines by opponents of pretribulationism. Biblical scholar Dr. Renald Showers defines and describes imminence as follows:

> 1) An imminent event is one which is always "hanging overhead, is constantly ready to befall or overtake one; close at hand in its incidence." ("imminent," *The Oxford English Dictionary*, 1901, V, 66.) Thus, imminence carries the sense that it could happen at any moment. Other things *may* happen before the imminent event, but nothing else *must* take place before it happens. If something else must take place before an event can happen, then that event is not imminent. In other words, the necessity of something else taking place first destroys the concept of imminency.

2)   Since a person never knows exactly when an imminent event will take place, then he cannot count on a certain amount of time transpiring before the imminent event happens. In light of this, he should always be prepared for it to happen at any moment.

3) A person cannot legitimately set or imply a date for its happening. As soon as a person sets a date for an imminent event he destroys the concept of imminency, because he thereby is saying that a certain amount of time must transpire before that event can happen. A specific date for an event is contrary to the concept that the event could happen at any moment.

4)   A person cannot legitimately say that an imminent event will happen soon. The term "soon" implies that an event *must* take place "within a short time (after a particular point of time specified or implied)." By contrast, an imminent event *may* take place within a short time, but it does not *have* to do so in order to be imminent. As I hope you can see by now, "imminent" is not equal to "soon."[2]

The fact that Christ could return soon at any moment (but may not) is a support for pretribulationism. What New Testament passages teach this truth of imminency? Passages that teach this truth are those stating that Christ could return at any moment without warning, and those instructing Christians to wait and look for the Lord's coming. Such passages include:

- 1 Corinthians 1:7—". . . awaiting eagerly the revelation of our Lord Jesus Christ."
- 1 Corinthians 16:22—"Maranatha."
- Philippians 3:20—"For our citizenship is in heaven, from which also we eagerly wait for a Savior, the Lord Jesus Christ."

- Philippians 4:5—"The Lord is near."
- 1 Thessalonians 1:10—". . . to wait for His Son from heaven."
- Titus 2:13—"looking for the blessed hope and the appearing of the glory of our great God and Savior, Christ Jesus."
- Hebrews 9:28—"so Christ . . . will appear a second time for salvation without reference to sin, to those who eagerly await Him."
- James 5:7–9—"Therefore be patient, brethren, until the coming of the Lord. . . . For the coming of the Lord is near. . . . Behold, the Judge is standing right at the door."
- 1 Peter 1:13—"Fix your hope completely on the grace to be brought to you at the revelation of Jesus Christ."
- Jude 21—". . . waiting anxiously for the mercy of our Lord Jesus Christ to eternal life."
- Revelation 3:11; 22:7, 12, 20—"'I am coming quickly!'"
- Revelation 22:17, 20—"The Spirit and the bride say, 'Come.' And let the one who hears say, 'Come.'. . . He who testifies to these things says, 'Yes, I am coming quickly.' Amen. Come, Lord Jesus."

In considering the passages above, we note that Christ may come at any moment, that the rapture is actually imminent. Only pretribulationism can give a full, literal meaning to such an any-moment event. Other rapture views must redefine imminence more loosely than the New Testament allows.

If the tribulation must occur first, as some believe, then the exhortation of Titus 2:13 that Christians are to be "looking for the blessed hope and the appearing of the glory of our great God and Savior, Jesus Christ" is greatly diminished. In such an interpretation, Christians should be looking for signs of Christ's coming rather than His coming. If the pretribulational view of imminence is not accepted, then it would make sense to look for signs related to events of the tribulation (i.e., the Antichrist, the two witnesses, etc.) and not for Christ Himself. But the New Testament, as demonstrated above, uniformly instructs the church to look for the coming of Christ—as opposed to tribulation saints who are told to look for signs.

The New Testament exhortation to be comforted by the Lord's coming (John 14:1; 1 Thess. 4:18) would no longer have meaning if Christians first had to pass through any part of the tribulation. Instead, comfort would have to await passage through the events of the tribulation. The church has been given a "blessed hope," in part, because our Lord's return is truly imminent.

The early church had a special greeting for one another, as recorded in 1 Corinthians 16:22, which was "Maranatha!" Maranatha consists of three Aramaic words: *Mar* ("Lord"), *ana* ("our"), and *tha* ("come"), meaning "our Lord, come." No wonder these ancient Christians coined such a unique greeting which reflects an eager expectation of the blessed hope as a very real presence in their everyday lives. The life of the church today could only be improved if "Maranatha" were to return as a sincere greeting on the lips of an expectant people. Maranatha!

PART 3

What Does the Bible Teach About the Tribulation?

Almost everyone has experienced turbulent and traumatic times during which there was great uncertainty or perhaps even enormous pain and sorrow. Such times are often periods of individual, familial, and perhaps even national crisis in which every personal, physical, and emotional resource is called into action in order to successfully endure the problem. Sorrow, grief, persecution, tragedy, catastrophe, famine, war, and uncertainty are all very real dynamics in daily life and newspaper headlines. However, according to the Bible, there will be a future time of even greater agony known as the "tribulation." This era will come after the rapture of the church and will be the greatest period of suffering the world has known. It will be the ultimate "future shock."

Wall Street's economic forecasters and speculators are often divided into optimists and pessimists, or "bulls" and "bears," based upon their "reading" of economic indicators and trends. In this same sense, interpreters of the Bible can read its prophetic passages and understand much of God's plan for the future. The difference with prophecy is that through careful and prayerful study, much of the speculation can be removed. Unlike tomorrow's markets, God's plan is clear and certain. Does belief in the rapture necessitate that

Christians be pessimistic and apathetic? Certainly not! We are to be realistic and anxious. We are realistic about the future and we are anxious and expectant about the coming of the Lord Jesus Christ for His church. We also however acknowledge that once the rapture occurs there will be a time of intense worldwide tribulation.

The Bible has more to say about these seven years of tribulation than any other prophetic time period. During this period of seven years, the Antichrist will emerge, persecution of new Christians and the Jewish people will ensue, and the great battle of Armageddon and the second coming of Christ will transpire.

The New Testament teaches that the current church age will also include trials and tribulation. Jesus said, "In the world you have tribulation, but take courage; I have overcome the world" (John 16:33). The Apostle Paul warned, "Indeed, all who desire to live godly in Christ Jesus will be persecuted" (2 Tim. 3:12). However, the world's persecution of the church in this age is not the wrath of God. The future tribulation will be a time of God's wrath upon a Christ-rejecting world, which the church has been promised by our Lord to be exempted from (Rev. 3:10).

Christians can daily live in confidence that human history will end with Jesus Christ as the victor. The future is certain. Yet Jesus told his disciples that before the final victory, "there will be a great tribulation, such as has not occurred since the beginning of the world until now, nor ever will" (Matt. 24:21). In its intensity and agony, it will be unfortunate and undesirable. But its certainty and course is not unforeseen or unpredicted. The Bible says that it will be tragic, but true.

15. What is the tribulation?

The tribulation in Bible prophecy is the period of time between the rapture of the church and the second coming of Jesus Christ. The most extensive biblical comments on the tribulation are found in the writings of John, specifically in Revelation 6–19. In these chapters, John provides a detailed exposition of the tribulation days. Daniel's Seventy Weeks, prophesied in Daniel 9:24–27 are the framework within which the tribulation, or the Seventieth Week, occurs. The seven-year period of Daniel's Seventieth Week provides the time span with which a host of descriptive terms are associated. Some of those terms include: "tribulation," "great tribulation," "day of the Lord," "day of wrath," "day of distress," "day of trouble," "time of Jacob's trouble," "day of darkness and gloom," and "wrath of the Lamb."

16. Where does the Bible teach about the tribulation?

There are numerous passages that teach that there will be a future tribulation period after the rapture.

Old Testament Passages

Throughout the Bible there are many direct and indirect references to the tribulation.[1] One of the first and earliest Old Testament passages to prophesy of this period is found in Deuteronomy 4:27–31. These verses foretell both the scattering of the Jews and their restoration to the Lord if they seek Him.

Before Israel had set foot in their promised land, the Lord foretold an outline of their entire history included in Deuteronomy. Their destiny is said in 4:30 to be a time of "distress" or "tribulation" (KJV) "in the latter days" right before Israel "will return to the LORD your God and listen to His voice." Later in Deuteronomy, Moses expands upon this time of tribulation and notes that its purpose will include a time of retribution to the Gentiles for their ill treatment of the Jews. Note Deuteronomy 30:7: "The LORD your God will inflict all these curses [Deut. 28] on your enemies and on those who hate you, who persecuted you."

Continuing along the same line, Isaiah 26:20–21 notes that the tribulation includes the purpose of punishing the nations of the earth for their sin. He also labels the tribulation an "indignation" from which Israel was to hide herself. Isaiah continues to describe the Lord's wrath and judgment in the tribulation on behalf of Israel in Isaiah 34:2–3, 8.

In the preaching of Jeremiah there is also reference to the tribulation. Not only did Jeremiah predict the Babylonian captivity of the Jews, he also foretold of a time of yet future trials for Israel. In Jeremiah 30:5–9, we read of this time, which is often known as "the time of Jacob's trouble."

One of the most important passages for the study of the future is Daniel 9:24–27:

> Seventy weeks have been decreed for your people and your holy city, to finish the transgression, to make an end of sin, to make atonement for iniquity, to bring in everlasting righteousness, to seal up vision and prophecy and to anoint the most holy place. So you are to know and discern that from the issuing of a decree to restore and rebuild Jerusalem until Messiah the Prince there will be seven weeks and sixty-two weeks; it will be built again, with plaza and moat, even in times of distress. Then after the sixty-two weeks the Messiah will be cut off and have nothing, and the people of the prince who is to come will destroy the city and the sanctuary. And its end will come with a flood; even to the end there will be war; desolations are determined. And he will make a firm covenant with the many for one week, but in the middle of the week he will put a stop to sacrifice and grain offering; and on the wing of abominations will come one who makes desolate, even until a complete destruction, one that is decreed, is poured out on the one who makes desolate.

In these four verses Daniel provides a clear and concise framework for prophetic study. This is a critical passage for prophetic studies. A proper understanding of these verses provides students of prophecy scriptural signposts for biblical prophecy. From this passage we learn that the tribulation is a seven-year period, divided by the "abomination of desolation" into two three-and-a-half year periods. Since Daniel's Seventy Weeks are Seventy Weeks of years, the final week of years (i.e., the tribulation) would thus be a seven-year period. (See the diagram and explanations in Question 20 for more details.)

Like Jeremiah, Daniel 12:1 calls this future period "a time of distress." In this verse, this time is described not just as "a time of distress," but also as a time when Israel "will be rescued."

The entire book of Joel is about the "day of the Lord," which is a synonym for "the tribulation." Notice a couple of citations from Joel that refer to the tribulation:

> Alas for the day!
> For the day of the LORD is near,
> And it will come as destruction from the Almighty. (1:15)

> Blow a trumpet in Zion,
> > And sound an alarm on My holy mountain!
> > Let all the inhabitants of the land tremble,
> > For the day of the LORD is coming;
> > Surely it is near,
> A day of darkness and gloom,
> > A day of clouds and thick darkness
> > As the dawn is spread over the mountains,
> > So there is a great and mighty people;
> > There has never been anything like it,
> > Nor will there be again after it
> > To the years of many generations. (2:1–2)

The prophet Amos, a shepherd from the Judean town of Tekoa, also prophesied about the tribulation in Amos 5:18–20, as did the prophet Zephaniah. Even though Zephaniah is one of the smallest books in the Bible, one of the most important passages relating to the tribulation is found there. The Lord, through Zephaniah, just about exhausts the thesaurus as He pours out a vivid description of the tribulation in Zephaniah 1:14–18. Some of the other Old Testament prophecies of this era include (and this is not exhaustive), Joel 2:28–32 and Isaiah 2:12–22; 24.

New Testament Passages

The New Testament, building upon an Old Testament foundation, expands our picture of the tribulation. The first extended passage to deal with the tribulation in the New Testament is Matthew 24:4–28 (see also Mark 13, Luke 17:22–37, and Luke 21:5–36 for parallel passages). In this discourse, Jesus describes for the disciples the tribulation period. In verses 4–14, He speaks about the first half of the tribulation, and in verses 15–28, He describes the second half leading up to the second coming. According to Jesus, the tribulation will be intense and extensive and will include both human and natural disasters. Jesus also told the disciples that the second half of the tribulation would be no better than the first half. In fact, the trauma and suffering would escalate to such a point that it would end only after the battle of Armageddon and the second coming of Christ.

Paul's Thessalonian Epistles have been characterized as the Pauline Apocalypse, since they deal extensively with the prophetic. Twice Paul refers to the tribulation when speaking of a future time of wrath (see also Rom. 5:9):

- 1 Thessalonians 1:10—"and to wait for His Son from heaven, whom He raised from the dead, that is Jesus, who rescues us from the wrath to come."
- 1 Thessalonians 5:9—"For God has not destined us for wrath, but for obtaining salvation through our Lord Jesus Christ."

In 2 Thessalonians 2:1–2, Paul tells his readers that they should not be deceived into thinking that the tribulation (i.e., the day of the Lord) had already started:

> Now we request you, brethren, with regard to the coming of our Lord Jesus Christ and our gathering together to Him, that you not be quickly shaken from your composure or be disturbed either by a spirit or a message or a letter as if from us, to the effect that the day of the Lord has come.

He then continued in verses 3–13 to expound on some of the events of the tribulation era.

The most extensive biblical comments on the tribulation are found in the writings of John, specifically in Revelation 6–19. In these chapters, John provides a detailed exposition of the tribulation days. An example of John's specific mention of the tribulation can be seen in Revelation 7:14:

> And I said to him, "My lord, you know." And he said to me, "These are the ones who come out of the great tribulation, and they have washed their robes and made them white in the blood of the Lamb."

These chapters in Revelation are rich in both imagery and content and leave little doubt in the reader's mind regarding the crisis that is yet to come.

The Great Tribulation and the Tribulation

We believe the Bible distinguishes between the tribulation period (seven years) and what is known as the great tribulation (the final three and a half years). In Matthew 24:9 the term *tribulation* most likely refers to the full seven-year period of the tribulation. On the other hand, Matthew 24:21 speaks of the "great tribulation," which begins with the abomination of desolation that takes place after the midpoint of the seven-year period (Matt. 24:15).

In Matthew 24:15–20, Jesus told His disciples that after the midpoint of the tribulation the Antichrist will break his covenant with Israel and that following this there will be an increase in persecution: "For then there will be a great tribulation, such as has not occurred since the beginning of the world until now, nor ever will" (Matt. 24:21).

Is the phrase "great tribulation" a technical phrase referring to the last three and a half years of the tribulation, or is it simply a descriptive term of those years? The Bible clearly teaches two segments, but does it label them differently? In other words, does the Bible itself label the first three and a half years as "the tribulation" and the second three and a half years as "the great tribulation" or are the terms "tribulation" and "great tribulation" synonyms for the entire seven-year era? Premillennial pretribulational interpreters are divided on how the term "great tribulation" is used in the Bible. However, *there is no doctrinal orthodoxy or major interpretive issue at stake for whichever view is taken.* For either view, the basic seven-year, two-segment tribulation remains. What changes is how those two segments of three and a half years are labeled. In a formula format, some understand:

SEVEN-YEAR TRIBULATION (3½ YEARS + 3½ YEARS) =
GREAT TRIBULATION (3½ YEARS + 3½ YEARS)

Others understand:

SEVEN-YEAR TRIBULATION (3½ YEARS + 3½ YEARS) =
TRIBULATION (3½ YEARS) + GREAT TRIBULATION (3½ YEARS)

Regardless of the view taken, both have a seven-year tribulation with two parts and both recognize an increase in intensity during the last three and a half years.

17. What is the purpose of the tribulation?

God's basic purpose for the tribulation is that it be a time of judgment, while at the same time holding forth the grace of the gospel, which will precede Christ's glorious thousand-year reign in Jerusalem from David's throne.

Dr. Arnold Fruchtenbaum divides God's purpose into three aspects,[2] summarized as follows:

- *To make an end of wickedness and wicked ones.* The first purpose for the tribulation is seen to be a punishment in history upon the whole world for its sins against God, similar to the purpose of the global flood in Noah's days (Matt. 24:37–39).

  Isaiah 13:9—"Behold, the day of the LORD is coming, cruel, with fury and burning anger, to make the land a desolation; and He will exterminate its sinners from it."

  Isaiah 24:19–20—"The earth is broken asunder, the earth is split through, the earth is shaken violently. The earth reels to and fro like a drunkard, and it totters like a shack, for its transgression is heavy upon it, And it will fall, never to rise again."

- *To bring about a worldwide revival.* This purpose is given and fulfilled in Revelation 7:1–17. During the first half of the tribulation, God will evangelize the world by the means of the 144,000 Jews and thus fulfill the prophecy found in Matthew 24:14.[3]

  Matthew 24:14—"This gospel of the kingdom shall be preached in the whole world as a testimony to all the nations, and then the end will come."

- *To break the power of the holy people—Israel.* Finally, the tribulation will be a time in which God, through evil agencies, prepares Israel for her conversion and acknowledgment that Jesus is her Messiah, resulting in the second coming of Christ. Fruchtenbaum notes:

  > In Daniel 11 and 12, the prophet was given a vision of what conditions will be like for his people (Israel) during the tribulation. Then in Daniel 12:5–7 a

question is raised as to how long this period will be allowed to continue.

> Daniel 12:5–7—"Then I, Daniel, looked and behold, two others were standing, one on this bank of the river, and the other on that bank of the river. And one said to the man dressed in linen, who was above the waters of the river, 'How long will it be until the end of these wonders?' And I heard the man dressed in linen, who was above the waters of the river, as he raised his right hand and his left toward heaven, and swore by Him who lives forever that it would be for a time, times, and half a time; and as soon as they finish shattering the power of the holy people, all these events will be completed."

This passage provides a third goal of the tribulation. It is to break the power or the stubborn will of the Jewish nation. The tribulation will continue and will not end until this happens. So from this, the third purpose of the tribulation can be deduced: God intends to break the power of the holy people in order to bring about a national regeneration.[4]

18. What are the major events of the tribulation?

The seven-year tribulation is divided into two three-and-a-half-year parts. We will look at the major events of each half and the events occurring in the middle, knowing that some can be placed in their proper sequence, while other events are harder to place. The following chart should give a helpful overview.

Seal, Trumpet, and Bowl Judgments

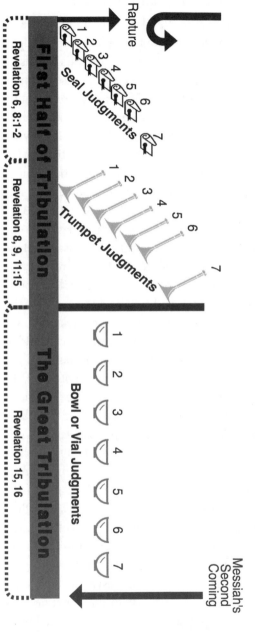

Rapture

Seal Judgments
1 2 3 4 5 6 7

Trumpet Judgments
1 2 3 4 5 6 7

Bowl or Vial Judgments
1 2 3 4 5 6 7

First Half of Tribulation

Revelation 6, 8:1-2

Revelation 8, 9, 11:15

The Great Tribulation

Revelation 15, 16

Messiah's
Second
Coming

Events of the First Half of the Tribulation

1. *The seal judgments.* Revelation 6 outlines the seven seal judgments (the seventh contains the trumpet judgments) that begin the tribulation.[5] The first four seals are also known as the four horsemen of the Apocalypse. These judgments are the beginnings of the wrath of God that is directed at the earth.

2. *The rise of Antichrist and the ten-nation confederacy.* Since the beginning of the tribulation will be marked by the signing of a covenant between Israel and the Antichrist (Dan. 9:26–27), it makes sense that he will come on the scene in the first half of the tribulation. He will be the head of a ten-nation confederacy (Dan. 2:42, 44; 7:7, 24; Rev. 12:3; 13:1; 17:12, 16) that will rule the world during the tribulation.

3. *The ministry of Elijah.* Malachi 4:5–6 says, "Behold, I am going to send you Elijah the prophet before the coming of the great and terrible day of the LORD. He will restore the hearts of the fathers to their children, and the hearts of the children to their fathers, so that I will not come and smite the land with a curse." The ministry of Elijah, which could be fulfilled through the ministry of the two witnesses (Rev. 11:3–6), will be one of restoration toward the nation of Israel. Since it will be "before the coming of the great and terrible day of the LORD," it will occur in the first half of the tribulation.

4. *The revival through the 144,000 Jewish evangelists.* Revelation 7 details the call and ministry of 144,000 Jewish evangelists who preach the gospel during the first half of the tribulation.

5. *The trumpet judgments.* Revelation 8, 9, and 11:15–19 speak of the trumpet judgments. As with the seal judgments, the seventh trumpet contains the final series of judgments known as the bowl judgments. These judgments focus on nature and include two of the three woe judgments.

6. *The ministry of the two witnesses.* Just as the 144,000 are engaged in world evangelism, the two witnesses are sealed by God (Rev. 11:3–6) to be a special witness to Jerusalem and Israel.

7. *The false church.* Also known as "Ecclesiastical Babylon," this false church will have great power and influence during the first half of the tribulation (Rev. 17:1–6). She will aid the Antichrist in his deception.

Events of the Middle of the Tribulation

1. *The little scroll.* The Apostle John is commanded by the interpreting angel to eat the scroll in Revelation 10:9–11. The content of the scroll is prophecy relating to the middle and second half of the tribulation. Biblical prophecy is considered good (i.e., sweet) by many people, but the message of judgment (i.e., bitter) is hard to take.

2. *The Antichrist is killed.* Revelation 13:3 notes that the seventh head (a reference to Antichrist) is killed. As we will note later, he is not yet finished.

3. *Satan cast down to the earth from heaven.* Revelation 12:7–9 reveals that Satan himself is cast to the earth from heaven through angelic agency. This provides the basis for an intensification of events upon the earth during the second half of the tribulation.

4. *The resurrection of the Antichrist.* One of the first things Satan does on the earth after being cast out of heaven is to resurrect the Antichrist. Revelation 13:3–4 records this episode as Antichrist attempts to counterfeit the career of Jesus, the Messiah.

5. *Three kings killed and seven submit.* After his death and resurrection, Antichrist consolidates his worldwide rule by killing three of the ten kings, which leads to the other seven submitting voluntarily. This event provides the political basis from which Antichrist will project his power during the last half of the tribulation (Dan. 7:24; Rev. 17:12–13).

6. *Destruction of the false church.* As has often been the case historically, when a tyrant reaches his goal of total political control he destroys those who helped him reach that point.

Antichrist now destroys the harlot, Ecclesiastical Babylon, as noted in Revelation 17:16.

7. *The death and resurrection of the two witnesses.* God enables the temporary deception of Antichrist to proceed further with the death of the two witnesses. During the first half of the tribulation, the two witnesses were miraculously protected by God. Now, God allows the deception of Antichrist to deepen when he murders the Two Witnesses in Jerusalem and the whole world rejoices. However, after three and a half days the two witnesses will be resurrected and taken to heaven in the sight of all. Fear then grips those who have followed after the Beast (Rev. 11:11–13).

8. *The worship of the Antichrist.* Since the "earth dwellers" prefer the counterfeit over the genuine, they will be deceived into worshipping the Antichrist as God. In reality they will be worshipping Satan (Rev. 13:3, 4, 8). No wonder the Bible is filled with warnings about spiritual deception!

9. *The rise of the False Prophet.* This person is a counterfeit of the ministry of the Holy Spirit in that he is temporarily empowered to do false signs, wonders, and miracles which greatly aid the Antichrist's rise to power (Rev. 13:11–15). False religion is the vehicle of deception for this second beast—the False Prophet.

10. *The mark of the Beast (666).* Another "ministry" of the False Prophet will be the administering of the counterfeit seal of the Holy Spirit, the famous mark of the Beast—666. Placement of this mark on the forehead or right hand will be required to conduct economic transactions during the second half of the tribulation. It should be noted that any person receiving this mark cannot be saved. This mark will not be distributed during the first half of the tribulation, but only during the latter half. Since the meaning of 666 is a mystery, it is not wise to speculate as to its meaning until the time in which it is distributed. It is clear that its meaning will be clear to believers during the tribulation (Rev. 13:16–18).

11. *The seven-year covenant broken.* It is not at all surprising that the Antichrist should break his covenant with Israel. Such a move is in keeping with his character. This betrayal will involve Antichrist's military invasion of Israel.

12. *The abomination of desolation.* Antichrist will not only break his covenant with Israel, he will set himself up as God to be worshipped in the rebuilt Jewish Temple at the midpoint of the tribulation. This defiling act of the Third Temple is called "the abomination of desolation." This will be a sign to the Jews to flee Jerusalem (Dan. 9:27; Matt. 24:15–16; 2 Thess. 2:4).

13. *The persecution of the Jews.* The second half of the tribulation will be characterized by an extreme attempt to wipe out the Jews from off the face of the earth. Likely, Satan's thinking on this matter is that if the Jews are exterminated then God's plan for history will have been thwarted. Satan might think that this would somehow prevent the second coming. This persecution is pictured in Revelation 12:1–6. Within the imagery, the woman represents Israel and her male child represents Christ.

Events of the Second Half of the Tribulation

1. *The bowl judgments.* The bowl judgments are the most severe series of judgments of the whole tribulation. They occur in the second half of the tribulation, devastate Antichrist's kingdom, and prepare the way for the second coming of Christ. The bowl judgments are the result of the prayers of the saints for God to take revenge on their behalf (Rev. 15:1–8). The bowl judgments are described in Revelation 16.

2. *The protection of the Jewish remnant.* At the midpoint of the tribulation the Jews will flee when the Antichrist commits the abomination of desolation. Apparently these Jews will be protected in the Jordanian village of Bozrah, known also as Petra. A remnant will be preserved through this and other means (Micah 2:12; Matt. 24:16; Rev. 12:6, 14).

3. *The conversion of Israel.* Just before the second coming of
Christ, Israel will be converted to the messiahship of Jesus
and saved from their sins. This will prepare them for their
role in the millennial kingdom after the second advent (Zech.
12:10; Rom. 11:25–27).

19. Why would present-day Christians want the Jews back in the land of Israel if so many of them are going to die in the tribulation?

Is belief in the tribulation inherently anti-Semitic? Is it dispensationalism's future holocaust? Some critics of pretribulationism
accuse its proponents of contributing to a future Jewish holocaust
because Zechariah 13:8–9 teaches that a third of the Jews will come
to faith in Jesus as their Messiah during the tribulation and be
killed for their faith.[6]

While it is true that many Jewish believers will die in the tribulation, it is also true that about three-fifths of the entire earth's population will be killed during the course of those seven years, many
of them believers (Rev. 6:9–11). It will be a time of horrific death for
millions of people regardless of their ethnicity.

One of the main purposes of the tribulation (the Seventieth
Week of Daniel) is to bring the nation of Israel to faith in Jesus
as their Messiah. Jewish believer Arnold Fruchtenbaum explains
God's purpose for His people during the tribulation as follows
when commenting on Ezekiel 20:34–38:

> God intends to break the power of the holy people in order
> to bring about a national regeneration. . . . In this passage
> Ezekiel draws a simile with the Exodus . . . What is impor-
> tant to note here is that after God gathers the Jews from
> around the world, He will enter into a period of judgment
> (tribulation) with them. The rebels among the Jewish peo-
> ple will be purged out by this judgment. Only then will the

whole new nation, a regenerate nation, be allowed to enter
the promised land under King Messiah.[7]

Because all unbelieving Jews will be purged out and killed by the
end of the tribulation—regardless of their geographical location on
planet Earth—it is inconsequential as to whether they are in Israel
or hide away in a remote place. At the second coming, all unbelievers will be killed and prevented from going into the millennium
(Matt. 13:36–43, 45–50; 25:31–46). The only ones (Jew or Gentile)
who will survive the tribulation will be those who have become
believers in Jesus as their Messiah.

Critics ask: "Why isn't [Tim] LaHaye [a pretribulationist and
coauthor of the *Left Behind* series of novels on prophecy] warning
Jews now living in Israel about this pre-determined holocaust by
encouraging them to leave Israel until the conflagration is over?"[8]
LaHaye and pretribulationists are not doing so because these
events cannot take place before the rapture. We agree that there
should be a warning. However, it will not be given to the Jews living in the land of Israel until the middle of the tribulation. In fact,
Matthew 24:15–16 says of that time, "Therefore when you see the
abomination of desolation which was spoken of through Daniel
the prophet, standing in the holy place (let the reader understand),
then those who are in Judea must flee to the mountains." The parallel passage in Revelation 12:6 says, "Then the woman fled into
the wilderness where she had a place prepared by God, so that
there she would be nourished for one thousand two hundred and
sixty days." The woman represents Israel, or even more precisely
the elect Jewish remnant, which are the Jewish elect that will obey
Christ's warning to head for the hills "when you see the abomination of desolation." This remnant will be divinely protected by God
in the wilderness until Christ returns physically to Jerusalem and
sends His angels to gather His elect (Matt. 24:31) for His approach-
ing kingdom.

As noted above, as part of the process of bringing the Jewish remnant to faith Zechariah 13:8 speaks of a purging out of the non-elect Jewish element from the nation. "'It will come about in all the land,' declares the LORD, 'that two parts in it will be cut off and perish; but the third will be left in it.'" The Old Testament prophets speak frequently of the purging out of the Jewish non-elect during the tribulation.

Ezekiel 20:33–38 is a major passage that speaks of a Jewish regathering to their ancient land. This regathering must take place before the tribulation, in preparation for the purging of the non-elect Israelites called in this passage "the rebels" (Ezek. 20:38). Two chapters later, Ezekiel receives another revelation about a future regathering of national Israel (Ezek. 22:17–22). This time, the Lord is "going to gather you into the midst of Jerusalem" (Ezek. 22:19). Like the metallurgist, the Lord will use the fire of the tribulation to purge out the unfaithful. The Lord is going to "gather you [Israel] and blow on you with the fire of My wrath, and you will be melted in the midst of it" (Ezek. 22:21). In this passage, "My wrath" depicts the time of the tribulation. It also follows here that the nation must be regathered before that event can take place. The outcome of this event will be that the nation "will know that I, the LORD, have poured out My wrath on you" (Ezek. 22:22). Israel is back in her land, awaiting the purging fire of the tribulation that will remove the non-elect and reveal the remnant. Other verses that address this time are Isaiah 1:22, 25; 48:10; Jeremiah 6:27–30; 30:7, 11, 22, 24; Daniel 12:1, 9–10; and Malachi 3:2–3.

The second coming is a rescue event. Jesus will return to the earth in order to rescue the believing Jewish remnant that is on the verge of being destroyed during the campaign of Armageddon. The Old and New Testaments teach that before Christ can return to the earth for His millennial kingdom the nation of Israel must be converted to Jesus as their Messiah and call on Him to save them (Lev. 26:40–42; Jer. 3:11–18; Hosea 5:15; Zech. 12:10; Matt. 23:37–39; Acts 3:19–21).

The Bible teaches that one day the nation of Israel will return to the Lord their God. This will occur by the end of the tribulation and is the purpose for the time of Jacob's trouble. Many passages teach the future conversion of the Jews to Jesus as their Messiah (Pss. 79:1–13; 80:1–19; Isa. 53:1–9; 59:20–21; 61:8–9; 64:1–12; Jer. 30:3–24; 31:31–40; 32:37–40; 50:4–5; Ezek. 11:19–20; 16:60–63; 34:25–26; 36:24–32; 37:21–28; Hosea 6:1–3; Joel 2:28–32; Zech. 9:11; 12:10–13:9; Rom. 11:25–27).

The Bible clearly teaches that the time of Jacob's trouble (the tribulation), in which the non-elect Jews are to be purged out and removed while the remaining believing remnant will be saved (both spiritually and physically), did not occur through events relating to the destruction of Jerusalem in A.D. 70. Fruchtenbaum says, "Only by faith in the Son of Man can Israel be regenerated. Only by calling upon the Name of the Lord can Israel be saved spiritually. Only by the return of the Son of Man can Israel be saved physically."[9] That is exactly what will occur in the tribulation.

20. What are Daniel's Seventy Weeks and how do they relate to the tribulation?

Daniel's Seventy Weeks, prophesied in Daniel 9:24–27, are the framework within which the tribulation (the Seventieth Week) occurs.[10] As noted earlier, the seven-year period of Daniel's Seventieth Week provides the time span to which a host of descriptive terms are associated. Some of those terms include: "tribulation," "great tribulation," "day of the Lord," "day of wrath," "day of distress," "day of trouble," "time of Jacob's trouble," "day of darkness and gloom," "wrath of the Lamb," etc. A graphic presentation of the seventy weeks assists greatly in understanding this intricate prophecy.

The chart of Daniel's Seventy Weeks presents a premillennial pretribulational perspective. That is, it shows the rapture occurring before the tribulation and the second coming of Christ occurring before the millennium. Although not all evangelicals hold to a pretribulational rapture (favoring instead a midtribulational or

Daniel's Seventy Weeks

(Daniel 9:24–27)

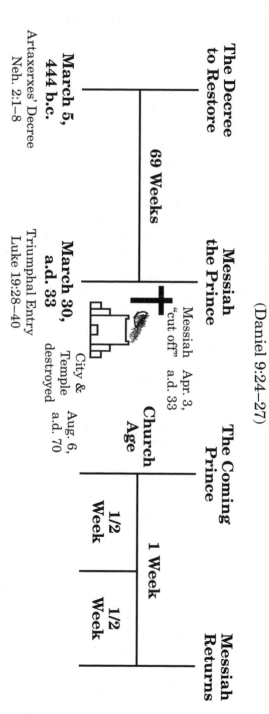

The Decree to Restore

March 5, 444 b.c.

Artaxerxes' Decree
Neh. 2:1–8

69 Weeks

Messiah the Prince

March 30, a.d. 33

Triumphal Entry
Luke 19:28–40

Messiah "cut off" Apr. 3, a.d. 33

City & Temple destroyed Aug. 6, a.d. 70

Church Age

The Coming Prince

1 Week

1/2 Week

1/2 Week

Messiah Returns

posttribulation view), there is agreement that the Antichrist will arise during the tribulation. He may be known, recognized, or even in power before the rapture, but he will only be revealed or manifested as Antichrist during the tribulation (2 Thess. 2:6, 8).

Explanation of Daniel's Seventy Weeks of Years

$$69 \times 7 \times 360 = 173,880 \text{ DAYS}$$
$$\text{MARCH 5, 444 B.C.} + 173,880 = \text{MARCH 30, A.D. 33}$$

Verification

$$444 \text{ B.C. to A.D. } 33 = 476 \text{ YEARS}$$
$$476 \text{ YEARS} \times 365.2421989 \text{ DAYS} = 173,855 \text{ DAYS}$$
$$+ \text{ DAYS BETWEEN MARCH 5 AND MARCH 30} = 25 \text{ DAYS}$$
$$\text{Totals} = 173,880 \text{ DAYS}$$

Rationale for 360-Day Years

Half week—Daniel 9:27
Time, times, half a time—Daniel 7:25, 12:7; Revelation 12:14
1,260 days—Revelation 12:6, 11:3
42 months—Revelation 11:2, 13:5
Thus: 42 months = 1,260 days = time, times, half time + half week
Therefore: month = 30 days; year = 360 days[11]

21. How does the Antichrist relate to the tribulation?

The Antichrist is the individual who arises during the tribulation and gains worldwide power for three and a half years. He is the imitator of the program of Jesus Christ and is known by many names throughout the Bible and discussed extensively in many passages.

Except for 1 John 2:22, the Bible never specifically refers to this coming leader as *the Antichrist*. It is a term that has been used by students of prophecy throughout church history to refer to him. The title *Antichrist* is clearly an appropriate term, for it captures the essence of the person and work of this individual. Among his many and more prominent identifications are the following:

- The little horn (Dan. 7:8)
- The insolent king (Dan. 8:23)
- The prince who is to come (Dan. 9:26a)
- The one who makes desolate, or, The abomination of desolation (Dan. 9:27c; Matt. 24:15)
- The man of lawlessness (2 Thess. 2:3)
- The son of destruction (2 Thess. 2:3)
- The lawless one (2 Thess. 2:8)
- The beast (Rev. 11:7; see also 13:1; 14:9; 15:2; 16:2; 17:3, 13; 19:20; 20:10)
- The despicable person (Dan. 11:21)
- The strong-willed king (Dan. 11:36)
- The worthless shepherd (Zech. 11:16–17)

According to Daniel 9:27, the Antichrist will emerge in power during the prophetic milestone known as the "Seventieth Week" and after the fulfillment of the previously prophesied sixty-nine weeks. After Christ returns and removes the Church from the earth, the Antichrist will ascend to power and as the "little horn" spoken of in Daniel 7:24–25, will lead a ten-nation confederation of western powers during the tribulation years. The Antichrist's future reign is certain but it will not commence until after the rapture occurs and the tribulation begins.

Two words describe the ascent of the Antichrist: *unification* and *subjugation*. According to Daniel 7:7–8 and 7:23–24, the Antichrist will rise to power after a confederation of ten nations emerges. This confederation is symbolized as a beast with ten horns and represents a final international political entity. It will be a unique and powerful empire. According to Daniel, "The fourth beast will be a fourth kingdom on the earth, which will be different from all the other kingdoms and will devour the whole earth and tread it down and crush it" (7:23).

The Antichrist will forcibly take control of the confederation and will subdue three of the ten members. "As for the ten horns, out of this kingdom ten kings will arise; and another will arise after them, and he will be different from the previous ones and will subdue three kings" (7:24). John writes of his ascent in Revelation 13:1: "And the dragon stood on the sand of the seashore. Then I saw a beast coming up out of the sea, having ten horns and seven heads, and on his horns were ten diadems, and on his heads were blasphemous names."

While the Antichrist emerges in a political environment and functions initially as a political leader, he also will gradually acquire religious connotations. Eventually he will require that those subject to him worship him when he sets up his image in Israel's Temple (2 Thess. 2:4).

The Antichrist will be a leader who pursues peace and wages war. In his pursuit of peace he will be both successful and deceitful, and in his waging of war he will be daring and destructive. He is often portrayed in the Bible as a warrior.

Once the Antichrist is in power and his program is fully manifested it will be all encompassing and intense. He will be active throughout all of the tribulation, but it is primarily the last half that will be tumultuous. His unprecedented, unparalleled, and unrestrained power will command worldwide attention for a period of forty-two months.

For three and a half years the Antichrist will persecute Christians and other opponents in a reign of terror that will dwarf all previous suffering and death experienced by humanity in previous persecutions, plagues, and pogroms. Once his mask as a man of peace is removed "the lawless one" (2 Thess. 2:8) will be revealed as a man of terror. This fits the historic pattern of satanic deception, which presents evil as good, a lie as the truth, and wickedness as righteousness.

According to the Bible, great armies from the east and the west will gather on the plain of Armageddon. There will be threats to the power of the Antichrist from the south and he will also move to destroy a revived Babylon in the east before finally turning his forces toward Jerusalem to subdue and destroy it. As he and his armies move on Jerusalem, God will intervene and Jesus Christ will return. The Lord will destroy the armies, capture the Antichrist and the False Prophet, and cast them into the lake of fire (Rev. 19:11–21).

When the Lord returns, the power and rule of the Antichrist will come to an end at the campaign of Armageddon. The second coming of Christ will crush the Antichrist and his armies and will bring forth a time of judgment (Rev. 19:20–21; 20:11–15). The Antichrist and the False Prophet will be cast into the lake of fire. This will immediately precede the binding of Satan (Rev. 20:1–3) and the inauguration of the millennial reign of Christ on the earth (20:4–6).

According to Revelation 19:20, the Antichrist will be captured along with the False Prophet and will be among the first to be thrown into the lake of fire (cf. Rev. 20:14). The Antichrist will be finished in history (unlike Satan who will be bound for 1000 years and then released and judged after a final rebellion). In all of his actions and attitudes, the Antichrist will indeed be *against* Christ, but it will be Christ, and not His human enemy, who will have the final victory.

22. What is the mark of the beast and who has it?

Scriptural references to the mark of the beast are found in Revelation 13:16–18; 14:9–11; 16:2; and 20:4.[12] The purpose of the mark is for commerce and worship, and every person who receives the mark will receive the same kind of mark. According to Revelation 13:16–18, during the tribulation, every person will be required to receive the "mark" (Greek, *charagma*) or name of the beast before "buying or selling"—that is, before they can conduct any business transactions. All private and public transactions will require that the parties have this mark. Those who do not have it will be subject to great difficulty, persecution, and death.

According to Revelation 13:16, the mark, a sign of allegiance, touches every part of society. John uses three couplets to emphasize this: the small and the great, the rich and the poor, and the free and the slaves. Every cultural category and subgroup of humanity will be affected. There are no favorites before the god of the satanic realm, and no distinction is made between the haves and the have-nots.[13]

Purpose of the Mark

Giving the mark will be a satanic counterpart to the "sealing" of believers by God in Revelation 7:2–4. Just as the 144,000 in chapter 7 are sealed upon their foreheads to receive divine protection, so in chapter 13 are unbelievers marked or sealed to receive the affirmation and protection of the Antichrist.

The word used for "seal" is not the same as the word used for "mark." Like everything else the Antichrist does, the mark of the beast is an imitation and mockery. It may also be a parody of the command by God in Deuteronomy 6:8 for the Jews to place the *Shema* on their hand and foreheads (though they were on the left rather than the right hands). Additionally, in Ezekiel 9:4, God required that the Hebrew letter *tau* be placed on the foreheads of all who repented of the nation's idolatry. This signified that those people once again belonged to God. So here in Revelation we see another imitation, parody, or mocking of God's actions by Satan.

To take the mark of the beast will signify one's commitment and devotion to the Antichrist, affirming the wearer's belief that Satan, rather than God, is the supreme deity. The mark will be a visible symbol (*on* the individual) of the immense power and worldwide authority and control of the Antichrist. According to Revelation

20:4, thousands of people will refuse to receive the mark and, as a result, will be beheaded. These tribulation martyrs will be resurrected at the second coming of Christ and the end of the tribulation and will reign with Him during the millennium.

The Nature of the Mark

The biblical word for *mark* is similar in meaning to the contemporary words *tattoo* or *brand*. Throughout the Bible, the word for *mark* is used to distinguish or indicate something by a sign. For example, it is used many times in Leviticus as a reference to a mark that renders the subject ceremonially unclean (see Lev. 13:47–59; 14:34–39). In such instances, it is usually related to leprosy. Ezekiel 9:4 uses the word *mark* much as it is used in Revelation: "The LORD said to him, 'Go through the midst of the city, even through the midst of Jerusalem, and put *a mark on the foreheads* of the men who sigh and groan over all the abominations which are being committed in its midst'" (emphasis added). In this instance, the mark was one of preservation, similar to the way the blood of the Passover lamb on the doorposts spared the Israelites from the death angel (Exod. 12:21–30). In Ezekiel the mark is placed on the forehead, which anticipates John's use of the term in Revelation.

All seven instances of the Greek word for *mark* occur in Revelation and refer to "the mark of the beast." Scholars have offered numerous and diverse suggestions for the nature of the mark, including an official stamp, a wearing of phylacteries, the letter *X* corresponding to the Greek letter that begins the name of Christ, an invisible mark (or some technological variation such as a microchip implant), and a branding implant.

Religious tattooing was widespread in the Roman Empire and the ancient world, and devotees of a particular god or goddess were often branded or marked to show their devotion. Third Maccabees 2:29 speaks of Ptolemy Philopator (reigned 222–205 B.C.) marking Jews with an ivy leaf mark, the mark of Dionysiac worship. The word for *mark* was also used for the image or name of the emperor on Roman coins, as well as for the seals that were attached to official documents.[14]

The Number 666

The apostle John states in Revelation 13:17 that the mark is "the name of the beast or the number of his name." In verse 18, John writes, "the number is that of a man; and his number is six hundred and sixty-six." The number is that of the Antichrist's name and the numerical value is that of 666. John begins the verse by stating "Here is wisdom"—that is, understanding and skill are necessary to solve the problem of the number. In a similar manner, Daniel was given instruction and insight into solving the enigmatic number 70 in relation to the prophetic 70 weeks (Dan. 9:22–27; see also 12:10). So too, during the tribulation, believers will receive insight and understanding in order to unravel the mystery of the number.[15]

Probably no other number in the Bible or in history has received as much attention and speculation as 666. There have been numerous competing historic and contemporary solutions for the identification and understanding of the mark and the number, including: (1) the names of various world leaders such as the popes, different Roman emperors, Adolf Hitler, Benito Mussolini, and even Henry Kissinger; (2) chronological calculations attempting to link the duration of the Antichrist's reign with an empire, religion, or nation such as Rome, Islam, or Nazi Germany; (3) apocalyptic riddles that use symbolism and contrast the name of Jesus with the number of the beast; and (4) a symbol for the Antichrist and his forces in which 666 symbolizes rebellion and imperfection.[16]

Some commentators of Revelation (including recent preterist interpreters), rejecting a futurist interpretation of the book, have argued that the individual referred to was Nero Caesar. The Latin form of his name, transliterated to Hebrew, adds up to 616. However, this view is contrary to the text which says "666," requires using a defective spelling, and lacks historical support.[17]

The Bible does not identify the Antichrist or interpret the

number. Instead, it says that when the Antichrist is revealed during the tribulation, the number of his name—the name's equivalent in numbers—will be 666. Any speculation as to the identity of the Antichrist before he is revealed goes beyond the bounds of legitimate principles of prophetic interpretation. The identification is simply not yet available.

When the Antichrist is revealed, the interpretation of the mark will come as a result of understanding five successive comments stated by John in Revelation 13:16–18: the name of the beast, the number of his name, the number of the beast, the number of a man, and the number 666. Following this logical progression, the number is the Antichrist's own name, that has a numerical value of 666.[18]

The practice of associating numerical values with names and letters is part of an ancient practice called *gematria*. In Hebrew, letters of the alphabet were also used as numbers in counting. The Hebrew alphabet has twenty-two letters, and in the use of gematria, the first nine letters corresponded to the numbers one through nine and the next nine letters corresponded to ten through ninety, and the last four letters to one hundred through four hundred. Every Hebrew name or word had a numerical significance.[19] The name of the Antichrist, when revealed in the future, will be the numerical equivalent of 666.

In summary, while the Bible does not completely identify the Antichrist or his mark, it does give some precise details about the mark. The mark of the beast will be:

1. the Antichrist's mark and identified with his person
2. the actual number 666 and not a representation
3. a mark like a tattoo, visible to the naked eye
4. *on* the person, as opposed to *in* him or her
5. easily recognized and not questioned
6. received voluntarily and not given through trickery or stealth
7. used after the rapture and not before it

8. used during the second half of the tribulation
9. necessary for conducting commercial transactions
10. universally received by non-Christians and rejected by Christians
11. a sign of worship and allegiance to the Antichrist
12. promoted by the false prophet
13. a mark that leads to eternal punishment because its wearers are non-Christians

The use of this mark by the Antichrist will be one of many attempts to mimic the importance, rule, and work of Jesus Christ during the tribulation. In that regard, it is interesting to note the words of the apostle Paul in Galatians 6:17: "From now on let no one cause trouble for me, for I bear on my body the brand-marks of Jesus."

23. What are the seal, trumpet, and bowl judgments?

The seal, trumpet, and bowl judgments are three series of seven judgments that occur during the tribulation. The seal and trumpet judgments happen during the first half of the tribulation and the bowl judgments come during the second half of the tribulation.

A natural reading of the book of Revelation will lead one to believe that the seal, trumpet, and bowl judgments of the tribulation are different from one another and occur in the sequence as presented in the text. However, a few prophecy teachers think that the seal, trumpet, and bowl judgments are not twenty-one different judgments, but only seven events that are described three times: first as seals, second as trumpets, and third as bowls.

We believe that the order of the seal, trumpet, and bowl judgments should be understood sequentially for the following reasons. First, this is the order in which they appear in the text and there are no specific reasons to suggest that they should be taken in a way different from how they are presented. Second, the details of each judgment are significantly different so that it is impossible to explain how each is a restatement of another. Third, out of the seventh seal and trumpet judgment arise the next set of judgments, while the seventh bowl judgment is an actual judgment. Thus, the seventh judgments cannot be harmonized within a recapitulation framework. Fourth, ordinal numbers are used in each sequence, i.e., first, second, third, etc., that indicate succession and not recapitulation. The specific textual details can only be harmonized if the judgments occur sequentially.

Seal Judgments

The first of three series of seven judgments that take place during the tribulation are the seal judgments (Rev. 6; 8:1). Seals in the ancient world were used to close up a scroll of writing, not to be opened until it reached the individual to whom it was sent. Seals were usually made by dripping hot wax on the papyrus and then pressing one's signet ring into the wax. A thorough study of Revelation 5 indicates that the scroll that was sealed is apparently the title deed of ownership to the earth. Only Jesus Christ—the Lamb of God—is found worthy to open the seal and commence with prosecution of the judgments of the tribulation. Each judgment proceeds once the Worthy One opens the seal.

- *First Seal Judgment* (Rev. 6:1–2). The first seal judgment is also called "the white horse judgment" (see question 24 below for more discussion). This first judgment is what we would call today a "cold war" and its rider is the Antichrist.
- *Second Seal Judgment* (Rev. 6:3–4). The second seal judgment is also called the "red horse judgment," representing death and warfare.
- *Third Seal Judgment* (Rev. 6:5–6). The third seal judgment is also called the "black horse judgment" and represents famine and economic distress.
- *Fourth Seal Judgment* (Rev. 6:7–8). The fourth seal judgment is

also called the "ashen horse judgment" and represents death and massive population decimation.

- *Fifth Seal Judgment* (Rev. 6:9–11). The fifth seal judgment is one that never really takes place. When the seal is broken it results in the martyrs of the tribulation crying out to God for revenge upon those unbelievers who killed them on the earth. They are told that the time for vengeance has not yet come, but that it will. The passage also expects more martyrs for Christ to join those already in heaven. The martyrs' prayer of vengeance is finally answered in Revelation 16:4–7 during the third bowl judgment.

- *Sixth Seal Judgment* (Rev. 6:12–17). The sixth seal judgment is very severe. Six things happen: (1) a great earthquake; (2) the sun is blacked out; (3) the moon becomes like blood; (4) the stars fell to the earth; (5) the sky tears apart like a scroll; and (6) every mountain and island are moved out of their places. Rather than such events leading to repentance and prayer to God for deliverance, they lead to further rebellion against God.

- *Seventh Seal Judgment* (Rev. 8:1). The seventh seal judgment inaugurates the next series of seven judgments known as the trumpet judgments.

Trumpet Judgments

The second of three series of seven judgments that occur during the tribulation are known as "the trumpet judgments" (Rev. 8–9; 11:15). A trumpet was used in the ancient world to signal a special announcement or some major event that was about to happen. These judgments certainly qualify as major events. All the judgments are administered by special angels, and the movement is from heaven to the earth—clearly showing that it is God, not nature, that is the origin of these afflictions. Many of these judgments are similar to the ten plagues on Egypt recorded in Exodus 7–11. The seven trumpet judgments are:

- *First Trumpet Judgment* (Rev. 8:7). The first trumpet judgment is "hail and fire mixed with blood" that was thrown down upon the earth with the result that "a third of the earth was burned up, and a third of the trees were burned up, and all the green grass was burned up." Many have seen parallels with the Old Testament judgments of Sodom and Gomorrah (Gen. 19) and the sixth plague upon Egypt in the exodus (Exod. 9:22–26).

- *Second Trumpet Judgment* (Rev. 8:8–9). The second trumpet judgment involves something "like a great mountain burning with fire" thrown into the sea so that "a third of the sea became blood, and a third of the creatures, which were in the sea and had life, died; and a third of the ships were destroyed." This judgment has similarities to the first plague in Egypt (Exod. 7:14–25).

- *Third Trumpet Judgment* (Rev. 8:10–11). The third trumpet judgment saw "a great star" fall from heaven, "burning like a torch, and it fell on a third of the rivers and on the springs of waters." The star is named Wormwood (meaning "bitter") and could be an angelic entity since it has a proper name and stars are sometimes associated with angels (Job 38:7; Rev. 1:10). Many died from the bitter water.

- *Fourth Trumpet Judgment* (Rev. 8:12–13). The fourth trumpet judgment smites the heavens so that a third of the sun, moon, and stars are affected, resulting in a third diminishing of each. This judgment parallels the ninth plague on Egypt (Exod. 10:21–23). In association with this judgment comes an angelic announcement to the earth concerning the three remaining trumpet judgments.

- *Fifth Trumpet Judgment* (Rev. 9:1–12). The fifth trumpet judgment involves another star fallen to the earth from heaven, but this one, likely Satan himself, has the key to the bottomless pit that he opens and looses a great swarm of demonic locusts. These special creatures are permitted to torture people for five months, but those tortured are prevented from dying. This demonic locust invasion is also spoken of in Joel 2:1–11. It will be a terrible time to be an unbeliever.

- *Sixth Trumpet Judgment* (Rev. 9:13–21). The sixth trumpet judgment releases four angels who are specially created for this moment in history. They are tasked with killing a third of the earth's human population. These angels also command an angelic host of 200 million demons that go forth as horsemen to inflict death. They are clearly of a demonic origin. They, like the creatures for the previous judgment, come from the bottomless pit and are clearly not human. By this time, at least half of the earth's population will have died in only a few years. Scripture states that they "did not repent of the works of their hands, so as not to worship demons, and the idols . . ."
- *Seventh Trumpet Judgment* (Rev. 11:1–19). The seventh trumpet judgment is simply the seven bowl judgments that follow.

Bowl Judgments

The third of three series of seven judgments that take place during the tribulation is known as "the bowl judgments" (Rev. 16). These judgments, when compared to the seal and trumpet judgments, appear to be the most intense and severe. Bowls represent the accumulated wrath of God that will be poured out in all of its fury to prepare the way for Christ's second coming. It appears that these bowls have been collecting God's wrath, so to speak, for a long time. Now they are full and ready to be poured. The angels who administer these judgments in Revelation 15 and 16 are pictured as turning the bowls upside down to ensure that every last drop of God's wrath goes forth. Nothing is held back. Each judgment is specifically directed at an object of God's wrath:

- *First Bowl Judgment* (Rev. 16:1–2). This bowl judgment is poured "into the earth" and aimed specifically at those who have taken the mark of the beast. In some measure, it is a fulfillment of Revelation 14:9–11. The judgment is an affliction of grievous, malignant sores upon the human body.

- *Second Bowl Judgment* (Rev. 16:3). The next bowl judgment is poured "into the sea," turning the water to blood so that every living thing that was left alive from previous judgments was killed. The stench and disease that will result from this event is difficult to imagine.

- *Third Bowl Judgment* (Rev. 16:4–7). The third bowl judgment is poured "into the rivers and the springs of waters" so that all remaining fresh water is also turned to blood. The third bowl judgment is God's answer to the martyrs' prayer to be avenged (Rev. 6:10). This "water-to-blood" judgment is accompanied by two declarations from the administering angel: (1) this act is in retaliation for "the blood of the saints and prophets" who had died from persecution for standing for the truth; and (2) the righteousness of God is revealed in this act and in all His judgments. • *Fourth Bowl Judgment* (Rev. 16:8–9). This judgment is poured "upon the sun" so that an extraordinary heat goes forth and scorches people with fire. In the third bowl judgment the evaluation of heaven is that God is righteous and just to act this way. In this judgment the response of people on the earth is reported—and it is the opposite of heaven: "They blasphemed the name of God . . . and they did not repent, so as to give Him glory" (16:9).

- *Fifth Bowl Judgment* (Rev. 16:10–11). The next bowl judgment is poured out "upon the throne of the beast" so that his whole domain is darkened with a blackout. This is similar to the darkness experienced in Egypt during the ten plagues (Exod. 10:21–23). Apparently this is not a normal darkness but is accompanied with some kind of agony that will cause people to gnaw their tongues because of the pain. Once again the response is to blaspheme "the God of heaven because of their

pains and their sores; and they did not repent of their deeds"
(Rev. 16:11).

- *Sixth Bowl Judgment* (Rev. 16:12–16). The sixth bowl judgment is poured out "upon the great river, the Euphrates" so that its flow of water dries completely. This is to prepare the way for the kings of the east to come to the mountains of Israel for the battle of Armageddon. God is clearly baiting the Antichrist and drawing him into His trap, which was set for further and final judgment at the second coming. The absolute demonic character of the satanic trinity is revealed in this judgment. Scripture notes that they will use "signs" to entice the kings of the earth to gather for Armageddon. Psalm 2 and Joel 3:9–11 are parallel passages depicting the gathering of the world's armies for Armageddon.

- *Seventh Bowl Judgment* (Rev. 16:17–21). The last bowl judgment is poured out "upon the air" so that "flashes of lightning and sounds and peals of thunder" announce the greatest earthquake in the history of the world. This judgment apparently takes place in conjunction with the descent of Christ at the second coming. This judgment is also reported in Joel 3:14–17; Zechariah 14:4–5; and Matthew 24:29. This worldwide earthquake will cause Jerusalem to be split into three sections, preparing the way for millennial changes after the second coming. This is also the moment of Babylon's sudden destruction. Further, this global judgment is accompanied by 100-pound hailstones from heaven. Once again the response of the unbelievers of the world is to blaspheme "God because of the plague of the hail, because its plague was extremely severe" (Rev. 16:21).

24. What and who are the four horsemen?

The first four seal judgments of Revelation 6:1–8 are depicted as riders on various colored horses—thus the four horsemen. The

first horse is white, the second red, the third black, and the fourth
is ashen or pale.

White Horse Judgment

The first horse and seal judgment is the white horse (Rev. 6:1–
2). The interpretation of this rider is greatly debated between two
major views. The first is that it represents Christ, and the second is
that it represents the Antichrist. Even though Christ does return in
Revelation 19:11 on a white horse, that does not mean that Christ
is pictured here. The second view is more likely, since one who
comes riding a white horse pictures a military conqueror. It is the
Antichrist who comes conquering at the beginning of the tribulation, which this judgment denotes, and Christ who comes conquering the Antichrist at the end of the tribulation in Revelation 19.
Some scholars believe that this judgment is a parallel with Matthew
24:5.

Red Horse Judgment

The second horse and seal judgment is the red horse (Rev. 6:3–4).
The red color of the horse appears to indicate blood and death since
the passage says that "it was granted to take peace from the earth,
and that men should slay one another; and a great sword was given
to him" (6:4). Some scholars believe that this judgment is a parallel
with Matthew 24:6–7a.

Black Horse Judgment

The third horse and seal judgment is the black horse (Rev. 6:5–
6). This rider came forth displaying "a pair of scales in his hand"
(v. 5), and saying, "A quart of wheat for a denarius, and three
quarts of barley for a denarius; and do not damage the oil and the
wine" (v. 6). A severe shortage of food is indicated. The monetary
description indicates that normal purchasing power will be reduced
to 1/8. Some scholars believe that this judgment is a parallel with
Matthew 24:7b.

Ashen (Pale) Horse Judgment

The fourth horse and seal judgment is the ashen horse (Rev. 6:7–8). This is the most severe of the four judgments in that "over a fourth of the earth is killed with sword and with famine and with pestilence and by the wild beasts of the earth" (v. 8). Some scholars believe that this judgment is a parallel with Matthew 24:7c.

25. What is Armageddon and how does it relate to the tribulation?

Armageddon will be the last great world war of history and will take place in Israel in conjunction with the second coming of Christ.[20] The battle, or more accurately, campaign of Armageddon is described in Daniel 11:40-45; Joel 3:9–17; Zechariah 14:1–3, and Revelation 16:14–16. It will occur in the final days of the tribulation, when, as John writes, the kings of the world will be gathered together "for the war of the great day of God, the Almighty" in a place known as "Har-Magedon" (Rev. 16:14, 16). The site for the converging of the armies is the plain of Esdraelon, around the hill of Megiddo. The area is located in northern Israel about twenty miles south-southeast of Haifa.

The term *Armageddon* comes from Hebrew. *Har* is the word for "mountain," and often appears with the Hebrew definite article "H." *Mageddon* is likely the ruins of an ancient city that overlooks the Valley of Esdraelon in northern Israel where the armies of the world will congregate.

According to the Bible, great armies from the east and the west will gather and assemble on this plain. There will be threats to the power of the Antichrist from the south and he will also move to destroy a revived Babylon in the east before finally turning his forces toward Jerusalem to subdue and destroy it. As he and his armies move on Jerusalem, God will intervene and Jesus Christ will return to rescue His people Israel. The Lord and His angelic army will destroy the armies, capture the Antichrist and the False Prophet, and cast them into the lake of fire (Rev. 19:11–21).

The Battle of Armageddon

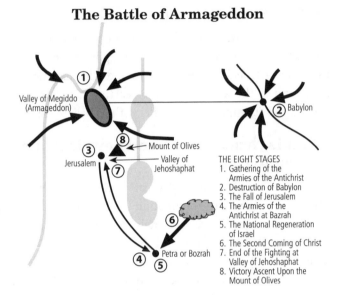

Valley of Megiddo (Armageddon)

① Babylon

Mount of Olives

③ Valley of
Jerusalem   Jehoshaphat
⑦

⑥

Petra or Bozrah
④ ⑤

THE EIGHT STAGES
1. Gathering of the Armies of the Antichrist
2. Destruction of Babylon
3. The Fall of Jerusalem
4. The Armies of the Antichrist at Bazrah
5. The National Regeneration of Israel
6. The Second Coming of Christ
7. End of the Fighting at Valley of Jehoshaphat
8. Victory Ascent Upon the Mount of Olives

26. What happens at the end of the tribulation and why does it all matter today?

Armageddon culminates in the second coming of Jesus Christ to the earth and the destruction of the forces of the Antichrist. This will conclude the seven-year tribulation. There will then be a seventy-five day transition period between the tribulation and the 1000-year reign of Jesus Christ upon the earth known as the millennium.

According to Daniel 12:11–12, mention is made of 1,290 days from the midpoint of the tribulation: "And from the time that the regular sacrifice is abolished, and the abomination of desolation is set up, there will be 1,290 days. How blessed is he who keeps waiting and attains to the 1,335 days!"

An extra thirty days are added to the normal three and a half years or 1,260 days, giving a total of 1,290 days. The extra thirty days added to the forty-five days (1335 – 45 = 1290) comes to a total of seventy-five days. This will likely be the time in which the sheep and goat judgment of Matthew 25:31–46 takes place and perhaps will also be additional time for setting up the millennium due to the devastation of the tribulation.[21]

During this interim period the image of the Antichrist that was set up in the temple at the middle of the tribulation will be removed after thirty days (Dan. 12:11). According to Revelation 19:20, the Antichrist and the False Prophet will be cast into the lake of fire at this point. Since the Antichrist was killed at the second coming of Christ, he will be resurrected for this punishment. Satan will also be bound at this time for the duration of the millennium (Rev. 20:1–3). During this time, Jewish survivors of the tribulation will be judged (Ezek. 20:34–38) as well as living Gentiles and the nations who are judged on the basis of their treatment of the Jews during the tribulation (Joel 3:1–3; Matt. 25:31–46). This will also be the time of the resurrection of Old Testament saints (Isa. 26:19; Dan. 12:2) and the resurrection of tribulation saints (Rev. 20:4–6).

Following this interval will be the millennial kingdom of Jesus Christ as foretold in passages such as Isaiah 2:2–4; Ezekiel 37:1–13; 40–48; Micah 4:1–7, and Revelation 20. In Psalm 2:6–9, the psalmist tells of the yet future reign of Jesus Christ:

> "But as for Me, I have installed My King upon Zion, My holy mountain. I will surely tell of the decree of the LORD: He said to Me, 'You are My Son, today I have begotten You. Ask of Me, and I will surely give the nations as Your inheritance, and the very ends of the earth as Your possession. You shall break them with a rod of iron, You shall shatter them like earthenware.'"

An earthly kingdom with a physical presence and rule by the Messiah-King is foretold throughout the pages of the Bible. This promise was not fulfilled in the first coming of Jesus Christ because, though offered, the kingdom was rejected by Israel and thus postponed until the second coming of Christ. Revelation 5:19 says that Christ is worthy to receive this kingdom, and in Revelation 11:15

we are told that the prophecies will yet be fulfilled. The millennium is a transitional period in God's program in that it is the beginning of the eternal rule of God in the kingdom, which will pass into the eternal state.

Human history has been filled with personal, national, and international tragedy and despair. In every century, every empire, and every era there have been multiple manifestations of original sin, the Fall, and satanic activity. Passages of biblical prophecy (and other portions of Scripture) clearly teach that the future will bring a specific period of increased trauma and tragedy during which terror and tribulation will be both intense and international. This era will last for seven years and, following the battle of Armageddon, will culminate in the second coming of the Lord Jesus Christ to establish His millennial kingdom and reign on the earth. We believe that this tribulation era of destruction and persecution will follow the rapture of the church. However, such a belief does not alleviate contemporary Christians of daily responsibilities, evangelism, discipleship, or holy living. Tribulation is certain, but so is triumph. Concerning the tribulation, it is not the living of *those* days about which we need be concerned. Rather, it is the living of *these* days. "Therefore be careful how you walk, not as unwise men but as wise, making the most of your time, because the days are evil" (Eph. 5:15–16).

PART 4

What Does the Bible Teach About the Second Coming?

He will come again to judge the living and the dead." Throughout the centuries faithful Christians have pronounced these words and proclaimed this truth in the Apostles' Creed and a score of other creeds of Christian orthodoxy. Belief in the physical return of Jesus Christ to the earth is the historic and biblical position of Christianity throughout the ages. Its acceptance is a biblical affirmation; its denial a doctrinal aberration.

Though many may not realize its significance, the return of Jesus Christ to planet Earth is the most important event that will occur in the future. Grocery store tabloids routinely carry outlandish and exaggerated stories of "prophetic scoops" of Christ's return that have nothing to do with the truths of the Bible. Only in the Bible do we find the definitive source for knowledge of God's prophetic plan. The second coming of Jesus Christ is as certain as the historicity of His first coming. The Bible is not silent on events surrounding the return of Jesus Christ. We know a great deal about His return and through careful study of God's Word, we can gain an understanding of the future that can affect the way we live daily.

The future is not all gloom and doom. It holds trials of an unprecedented nature in human history, but it also contains the glorious return of Jesus Christ to establish His righteous reign in preparation for the eternal state. The history of the Old Testament era was one of expectation for the first coming of the Messiah. The history of the New Testament and our own era is one of expectation for the second coming of the Messiah. Such an expectation is voiced when we pray "Thy kingdom come, Thy will be done" (Matt. 6:10). His kingdom will come when Christ returns and all of creation will acknowledge Jesus Christ, the hope of history.

27. Where does the Bible teach about the second coming of Jesus Christ?

The second coming of Jesus Christ to the earth is the subject of many passages in both the Old Testament and the New Testament, including the following: Deuteronomy 30:3; Psalm 2; Isaiah 63:1–6; Daniel 2:44–45; 7:13–14; Zechariah 14:1–4; Matthew 24–25; Mark 13; Luke 21; Acts 1:9–11; Romans 11:26; 1 Thessalonians 3:13; 5:1–4; 2 Thessalonians 1:6–2:12; 2 Peter 2:1–3:17; Jude 14–15; Revelation 1:7; 19:11–21.

Throughout the Old Testament there are many passages that describe the second coming and events surrounding it. From these passages we learn of the reign of Christ upon the throne of David, the government and conditions of the millennial kingdom that follow the second coming, and the judgment Christ will bring when He returns.

As we turn to the pages of the New Testament we find additional information. While on the earth the first time, Jesus Christ taught much about the second coming. One vivid description occurred in response to questions the disciples asked about the event:

> For just as the lightning comes from the east and flashes even to the west, so will the coming of the Son of Man be. Wherever the corpse is, there the vultures will gather. But

> immediately after the tribulation of those days the sun will be darkened, and the moon will not give its light, and the stars will fall from the sky, and the powers of the heavens will be shaken. And then the sign of the Son of Man will appear in the sky, and then all the tribes of the earth will mourn, and they will see the Son of Man coming on the clouds of the sky with power and great glory. (Matt. 24:27–30)

Probably the most graphic portrayal of Christ's second coming is found in Revelation 19:11–21. In this extended passage Jesus Christ is described as leading a procession of angels and saints in heaven to claim the earth, destroy the armies of the world, and defeat the Antichrist and False Prophet. The passage shows that Christ's return will be one that entails great physical destruction and many deaths. For those who are not Christ's own, it will be a terrifying and terrible event.

28. What will happen after the second coming of Jesus Christ?

The return of Christ will be followed by a series of judgments and then the inauguration of the millennial kingdom and one-thousand-year reign of Christ upon the earth. Just as Noah's flood recorded in Genesis 6–8 was a bridge from the old world to the new, so the judgments at the second coming will be the cataclysmic hinge between our current era and the tribulation to the radically new conditions of the millennium. Thus, the second coming and the judgments that will accompany it are closely tied together. The judgments at the second coming initiate the schedule for the millennium. These judgments will clean up the mess of previous human history so that the reign of Christ can commence. Regarding the relation of these two events, Dr. Walvoord observes:

> The millennial kingdom is a major part of the second coming of Christ. It includes the destruction of the armies

gathered against God in the Holy Land (Rev. 19:17, 21), the capture of the Beast and the False Prophet and their being cast into the lake of fire (v. 20), the binding of Satan (20:1–3), and the resurrection of the martyred dead of the Tribulation to reign with Christ a thousand years (vv. 4–6).[1]

The following are the specific judgments that occur either right before, at, or shortly after, the second coming:

- Judgment of Babylon, the great harlot (Rev. 17–18; 19:2, 3)
- Judgment of the armies and nations at Armageddon (Rev. 19:11–21)
- Judgment of the Gentile nations (Joel 3:1–3; Matt. 25:31–46)
- Judgment of the Beast or Antichrist (Rev. 19:19, 20)
- Judgment of the False Prophet (Rev. 19:20)
- Judgment of Satan (Rev. 20:1–3)
- Judgment of Old Testament saints (Dan. 12:1–3)
- Judgment of tribulation saints (Rev. 20:4–6)
- Judgment of living Jews (Ezek. 20:34–38)

The second coming of Jesus Christ is important for us today because it affects our lives each and every day and the priorities we set for our lives. We know what the end of human history will be and how it will unfold. Knowing that just as the prophecies of the first coming of Jesus Christ were fulfilled two thousand years ago, so also will the prophecies of the second coming of Jesus Christ be fulfilled at some point in the future. Dr. Carl F. H. Henry writes:

No prophetic doctrine is more prominent in the New Testament than that of the promised personal return in great power and glory of the crucified, risen and now exalted Jesus. The certainty of Christ's second coming in the New Testament connects with the fact of his already accomplished first coming.[2]

Because of the first coming, we can be certain of the second coming. Such certainty gives hope, purpose, goals, security, perspective, understanding, and meaning to even the smallest segments of daily life.

The second coming also assures us that the wrongs of this world will one day be righted. Tyranny, injustice, and deceit will come to an end in the marketplace and the great halls of power. With the righteous reign of Jesus Christ, justice will prevail. The second coming of Christ has enormous personal, ethical, national, and international significance. It will be the greatest event of history and its consequences are universal and eternal.

Every major Christian affirmation and creed of Christians throughout the centuries has affirmed Christ's second coming. Christians have proclaimed recognition and acceptance of the second coming daily around the world for two thousand years.

The fact that there will be a second coming is a truth that affects every person who has ever lived or will ever live. It is not a Hollywood special-effects production, religious raving, psychological paranoia, or monastery mysticism. It is a spectacular reality that will one day occur. It cannot be avoided.

PART 5

What Does the Bible Teach About the Millennium?

Thy kingdom come. Thy will be done, on earth as it is in heaven." Countless times every day for almost 2000 years Christians around the globe have voiced this prayer modeling the one Jesus gave to His disciples as recorded in Matthew 6:9–13 and Luke 11:2–4. What is being requested with these words?

Throughout its history, the world has known many kingdoms, many dynasties, and many empires. They have risen and fallen, blowing across the pages of history like leaves on an autumn day. Some have been spectacular and adorned with splendor; others have enslaved and slaughtered their populations. Regardless of how they are remembered, they all share the same common denominator—they had human leaders. Even in our own day, many think that if we could just get the right people into political office then humanity would be free to reach its full potential.

There are many views of history and its relation to the future. Some people see it as cyclical, others look back wishfully to a "golden age." Some say it is progressing according to "laws of nature," others say it is digressing by those same laws. To all of this, the Bible gives a clear and certain answer to the questions of the future. History and human events *are* going somewhere and there will be a glorious future kingdom. The prayers of Christians will be answered and God Himself—in the Person of Jesus Christ, the second member of the Trinity—will reign and rule on the earth for 1000 years in the millennial kingdom. The best is yet to come!

29. Where does the Bible teach about the millennium?

If you look in an English Bible concordance for the word *millennium,* you will probably be disappointed not to find it there. There are many passages that teach about the millennium even though the word itself is not mentioned. The millennium is a biblical doctrine and theological concept derived from many passages. Like many English theological terms, millennium is derived from Latin. It refers to the length of time that the Bible says Messiah's kingdom will last upon the earth before the end of history. Dr. John Walvoord writes:

> The English word *millennium* comes from the Latin word *mille,* meaning "thousand." The Greek word for millennium comes from *chilias,* meaning "a thousand," and *annus,* meaning "year." The Greek term is used six times in the original text of the twentieth chapter of Revelation to define the duration of Christ's kingdom on the earth prior to the destruction of the old heavens and the old earth. Therefore, the word millennium refers to the thousand years of Christ's future reign on the earth that will precede eternity.[1]

Numerous Old Testament passages speak of a yet future time of true peace and prosperity for the righteous followers of God under the benevolent physical rule of Jesus Christ on the earth. Zechariah 14:9 tells of this time saying, "And the LORD will be king over all the earth; in that day the LORD will be the *only* one, and His name the *only* one" (emphasis added). The passage then continues in verses 16–21 to describe some of the millennial conditions. Even though the Bible speaks descriptively throughout about the millennial kingdom, it was not until the final book of Revelation that the length of Christ's kingdom is revealed.

Isaiah also foretold of this future era:

> Now it will come about that in the last days, the mountain of the house of the LORD will be established as the chief of the mountains, and will be raised above the hills; and all the nations will stream to it. And many peoples will come and say, "Come, let us go up to the mountain of the LORD, to the house of the God of Jacob; that He may teach us concerning His ways and that we may walk in His paths." For the law will go forth from Zion and the word of the LORD from Jerusalem. And He will judge between the nations, and will render decisions for many peoples; and they will hammer their swords into plowshares and their spears into pruning hooks. Nation will not lift up sword against nation, and never again will they learn war. (Isa. 2:2–4)

Several chapters later, Isaiah again writes of the millennium:

> And the wolf will dwell with the lamb, and the leopard will lie down with the young goat, and the calf and the young lion and the fatling together; and a little boy will lead them. Also the cow and the bear will graze; their young will lie down together, and the lion will eat straw like the ox. The nursing child will play by the hole of the cobra, and the weaned child will put his hand on the viper's den. They will not hurt or destroy in all My holy mountain, for the earth will be full of the knowledge of the LORD as the waters cover the sea. (Isa. 11:6–9)

Other extensive Old Testament passages include: Psalm 2:6–9;

Isaiah 65:18–23; Jeremiah 31:12–14, 31–37; Ezekiel 34:25–29; 37:1–6; 40–48; Daniel 2:35; 7:13–14; Joel 2:21–27; Amos 9:13–14; Micah 4:1–7; and Zephaniah 3:9–20. These verses are only a few of the scores of prophetic passages found regarding this subject before the first coming of Christ.

The New Testament also gives significant witness to this coming kingdom because continuity with the Old Testament vision of a future millennial kingdom is maintained. It is the millennial kingdom of which Jesus spoke during the Passover meal before being betrayed and crucified:

> And when He had taken a cup and given thanks, He gave it to them, saying, "Drink from it, all of you; for this is My blood of the covenant, which is poured out for many for forgiveness of sins. "But I say to you, I will not drink of this fruit of the vine from now on until that day when I drink it new with you in My Father's kingdom." (Matt. 26:27–29; see also Mark 14:25; Luke 22:18)

The most extensive New Testament passage regarding the millennium is Revelation 20, in which John describes a chronological sequence—the binding, rebellion, and judgment of Satan in the millennium. Some prophecy scholars also hold that Revelation 21:9–27 describes the New Jerusalem during the millennium. This is not likely since it refers to the eternal state that is supported by the sequential development of the text from the millennium in Revelation 20 to the eternal state in Revelation 21. Yet others hold a mediating position and see the passage as teaching the eternal habitation of resurrected saints during the millennium.[2]

The future kingdom of God will have two distinct phases, the millennium and the eternal state. However, the overwhelming emphasis of the Bible is upon the thousand-year reign of Christ in His future kingdom known as the millennium. The millennium is a biblical reality that is yet to be realized. According to the Bible, life on the earth will get better, but not before it gets worse in the seven-year tribulation.

30. What is the purpose of the millennium?

In Psalm 2:6–9, the psalmist tells of the yet future reign of Jesus Christ:

> "But as for Me, I have installed My King upon Zion, My holy mountain. I will surely tell of the decree of the LORD: He said to Me, 'You are My Son, today I have begotten You. Ask of Me, and I will surely give the nations as Your inheritance, and the very ends of the earth as Your possession. You shall break them with a rod of iron, You shall shatter them like earthenware.'"

An earthly kingdom with a physical presence and rule by the Messiah-King is foretold throughout the pages of the Bible. This promise was not fulfilled in the first coming of Jesus Christ because, though offered, the kingdom was rejected by Israel. Revelation 5 says that Christ is worthy to receive this kingdom and in Revelation 11:15 we are told that the prophecies will yet be fulfilled. Dr. Charles Ryrie writes:

> Why is an earthly kingdom necessary? Did He not receive His inheritance when He was raised and exalted in heaven? Is not His present rule His inheritance? Why does there need to be an earthly kingdom? Because He must be triumphant *in the same arena* where He was seemingly defeated. His rejection by the rulers of this world was on this earth (1 Cor. 2:8). His exaltation must also be on this earth. And so it shall be when He comes again to rule this world in righteousness. He has waited long for His inheritance; soon He shall receive it.[3]

There are at least three major purposes for the millennium:

1. To reward the faithful who will then reign with Christ (Luke 19:16–19; Rev. 20:4–6)
2. To redeem creation, reversing the divine curses of Genesis 3 so that once again the earth will be as it was in the garden of Eden (Rom. 8:19–22)
3. To recognize the promises of God made in the covenants with Abraham in Genesis 12:1–3 and 15:18–21 (promising descendants, land, and blessing), with David in 2 Samuel 7:12–16 (dynasty, right to rule, and political kingdom), and with the nation of Israel in Jeremiah 31:34 (forgiveness of sins, the indwelling Spirit, and a new heart)

Among the biblical titles in the New Testament for the millennium are:

- the kingdom of heaven (Matt. 3:2; 8:11)
- the kingdom of God (Mark 1:14)
- times of refreshing (Acts 3:19)
- the period of restoration of all things (Acts 3:21)
- the world to come (Heb. 2:5)
- a kingdom which cannot be shaken (Heb. 12:28)

The millennium is a transitional period in God's program. It is the beginning of the eternal rule of God in the kingdom, which will pass into the eternal state. It is "the consummating link between history and the eternal order."[4] History and current events are moving toward a final era that will be the pinnacle of God's plan. Apart from the millennium, Christ's second coming would be cataclysmic and a coming in judgment, but history would then end, without fulfilling biblical promises of the reign of Christ during a period of true peace, justice, and security. The millennium will be everything that the tribulation was not. It is the first phase of the kingdom of God, of which the second is the eternal state (Rev. 22:5).

31. Who will be in the millennium?

Only the redeemed will enter the millennium. At the end of the tribulation, the unsaved and those who have aligned themselves with the Antichrist will be destroyed. There will then follow the judgment of the Gentiles (or nations) and the judgment of Israel. The judgment of the Gentiles will allow the believers to enter the coming kingdom, and non-believers will be cast into the lake of fire (Matt. 25:31–46). The judgment of Israel will be similar in that those Jews who accept Jesus as Messiah will enter the kingdom and those who do not will be cast into the lake of fire (Ezek. 20:37–38).

Also in the kingdom will be tribulation believers who died during the tribulation and all those who were raptured at the time of Christ's appearing before the tribulation. The Bible does not specifically address the issue of tribulation children and infants entering the millennium. We know that people who are Christians will enter, and people who are not will not enter. We also know that children will be born in the millennium and will need to face the issue of accepting or rejecting Jesus Christ as they mature (Isa. 65:23; Jer. 30:30; 31:29; Ezek. 47:22; Zech. 10:8). Thus, there will be children in the millennium, though not all of our questions are answered directly. Dr. Walvoord writes of the children of those who enter the millennium that they

> will be subject to the later decision regarding their salvation. Likewise children who are born in the millennial reign will face decision about salvation as they grow up. As the Millennium unfolds, there will come into existence a large number of people who will merely profess salvation without having the reality. This will explain the evil in the Millennium and also the final rebellion at the end.[5]

History is indeed headed somewhere and those who experience the millennium will be in an environment unlike anything the earth has known since the garden of Eden.

32. What are the major events and who are the key personalities of the millennium?

The millennium does not begin on the first day after the second coming of Christ and the end of the tribulation. According to Daniel 12:11–12, there will be a period of seventy-five days after the end of the tribulation during which time judgments of the Antichrist, the False Prophet, and the Gentiles will take place (Matt. 25:31–46). Also during this time there will be the resurrection of Old Testament saints and the resurrection of martyred tribulation saints following the sequence or order of 1 Corinthians 15:20–24.

From the midpoint of the tribulation (the "abomination of desolation" as described in Daniel 9:27; Matthew 24:15; and 2 Thessalonians 2:4), until the end of the tribulation will be three and a half years or 1,260 days. The additional seventy-five days recorded in Daniel 12:11–12 is an interval between the end of the tribulation and the beginning of the millennium.[6]

The major events of the millennium are:

- the binding of Satan (Rev. 20:1–3)
- the final restoration of Israel to include . . .
  –Regeneration (Jer. 31:31–34)
  –Regathering (Deut. 30:1–10; Isa. 11:11–12:6; Matt. 24:31)
  –Possession of the land (Ezek. 20:42–44; 36:28–38)
  –Re-establishment of the Davidic throne (2 Sam. 7:11–16; 1 Chron. 17:10–14; Jer. 33:17–26)
- the righteous reign of Jesus Christ (Isa. 2:3–4; 11:2–5)
- the loosing and final rebellion of Satan at the end of the millennium (Rev. 20:7–10)
- the great white throne judgment and the second resurrection or judgment of unbelieving dead (Rev. 20:11–15)

As seen in passages above, the major figures of the millennium are Jesus Christ and Israel. Satan will be bound and the church and the nations (Gentiles) will be present and active, but the focus of prophetic revelation is on Israel and Christ—the Messiah-King. Israel's prominence is required in order to facilitate a literal fulfillment of its many Old Testament promises by the Lord. All of the redeemed of God will participate in the worship, blessings, and glories of the millennial kingdom as they prepare for life in the eternal state.

33. What are the characteristics of the millennium?

Many of the things that have eluded humans thus far in history finally will be present in the millennial kingdom—peace, joy, justice, and prosperity. The millennial kingdom will bring about harmony in all of creation. Some of the most graphic portrayals of the millennial kingdom are found in the prophecies of Isaiah. In chapters 11 and 35, Isaiah provides extensive comment on the physical aspects of the kingdom.

Physical and Environmental Characteristics

Ever since the fall of Adam and Eve in the garden of Eden, humanity and creation have been under the judgment and ramifications of original sin. The pollution of sin has affected all of humanity and all of creation. However, during the millennium there will be a partial lifting of the curse and ramifications of original sin. There will still be death and the complete effects of the fall will not be lifted until the creation of the new heaven and new earth in the eternal state after the millennium (Rev. 22:3).

In Isaiah 35:1–2, we read of some of the effects of the millennium on the environment:

> The wilderness and the desert will be glad, and the Arabah will rejoice and blossom; like the crocus it will blossom

profusely and rejoice with rejoicing and shout of joy. The glory of Lebanon will be given to it, the majesty of Carmel and Sharon. They will see the glory of the LORD, the majesty of our God.

There will be abundant rainfall in areas that today are known for dryness and, therefore, there will be plenty of food for animals (Isa. 30:23–24; 35:7).

As part of nature and the created order, animal life will also be affected. The predatory instincts and carnivorous appetites will cease in animals. The distinctions between "tame" and "wild" will be erased as all creatures live in harmony (Isa. 11:6–7).

Physical conditions for people will also be drastically improved. Just as in the days before the flood of Noah, people will live much longer and the birthrate will increase (Isa. 65:20). Many physical infirmities and health concerns will also be eradicated (Isa. 29:18; 33:24). The absence of sickness and deformity along with the increased life spans will create less variation between those in the millennium with mortal bodies and those with resurrected bodies. Dr. Paul Benware writes of these two groups:

> It must be remembered that not all participants in the millennial kingdom will have earthly, mortal bodies. Millions of believers from the Old Testament era, the Church Age, and the Tribulation will have resurrected, immortal bodies. But there is no reason to think that these two groups will not be relating to one another and interacting with each other during the Millennium. The resurrected Lord Jesus had no problems teaching and fellowshipping with His disciples during the forty days after His resurrection.[7]

In the midst of this enhanced environment and increased level of health, there will be an overall effect of increased prosperity as poverty, injustice, and disease cease (Jer. 31:12–14).

Unfortunately, even in the midst of such pristine conditions, there will ultimately be human rebellion. Because the complete effects of the fall will not be erased, there will be a final revolt against the righteous government of Jesus Christ. This will occur at the end of the millennium when Satan is briefly released from bondage just prior to his final judgment and destruction (Revelation 20:7–10).

Political Characteristics

The government and politics of the millennial kingdom will focus on the benevolent reign of Jesus Christ as Israel's Messiah-King. It will be a theocracy centered in Jerusalem (Isa. 2:1–4), where Jesus will reign as both Messiah and King of Israel fulfilling the promises and prophecies of the Davidic Covenant (2 Sam. 7:12–16). God's covenant with David guaranteed David's dynasty, throne, and kingdom would continue forever. When Jesus Christ returns at the end of the tribulation, He will reestablish the Davidic throne in His personal rule as described by the prophet Jeremiah (23:5–8) and His reign will fulfill the well-known prophecy of Isaiah 9:6–7.

Other significant passages describing Christ's reign over Israel include Psalm 2; Jeremiah 33:20–26; Ezekiel 34:23–25; 37:23–24; and Luke 1:32–33. These and other passages provide ample specific evidence that the kingdom promised to David will be fully realized in the future. Christ's rule will also extend to the Gentiles and all nations throughout the world. We know from Psalm 2:6–9 that Christ will rule over the entire earth and in Daniel 7:14 we are again told of Christ's universal rule.

One of the major consequences of the righteous and benevolent rule of Christ will be the extension of peace throughout the world. Throughout its history the world has been plagued with war and its effects. There has been no lasting peace, and every portion of the globe has suffered from the destruction of war. Only in the millennium will the words of Micah's prophecy of hammering swords into plowshares and spears into pruning hooks finally come true (Micah 4:3–4). True peace and true prosperity will ultimately be realized in the millennial kingdom. Those things that have been so elusive and fading throughout human history will be realized only in the reign and timing of the Lord Jesus Christ.

Spiritual Characteristics

Spiritual life in the millennial kingdom will be an experience unlike any previous era for the redeemed because of the presence of the exalted King—the Lord Jesus Christ. Living daily in the personal and physical presence of Jesus Christ will have enormous manifestations in the lives of believers. Isaiah states: "the earth will be full of the knowledge of the LORD as the waters cover the sea" (Isa. 11:9). The knowledge and worship of Christ will be global and unimpeded. There will be no persecution, no secret gatherings or underground assemblies, and no religious censorship. According to Revelation 20:1–3, Satan and his demonic forces will be bound and rendered inactive until the end of the millennium. His removal will greatly enhance the spiritual condition of the world that would otherwise be impeded and attacked.

The millennium will be an era of great spiritual awareness, sensitivity, and activity for both Christians and the restored nation of Israel. For Israel, the new covenant will be in effect with the resulting conditions prophesied in passages such as Isaiah 59:20–21; Jeremiah 31:31–34; 32:37–40; Ezekiel 16:60–63; and 37:21–28.

Just as in the present age, the ministry of the Holy Spirit will be present and will indwell all believers (Jer. 31:33; Ezek. 36:27; 37:14). In addition to the indwelling of the Holy Spirit, the filling of the Spirit will also occur (Isa. 32:15; 44:3; Ezek. 39:29; Joel 2:28–29). But, unlike the present age, evangelism will not be needed since everyone will know the Lord. (This is evidence that our current age is not to be equated to the millennium.)

Spiritual conditions in the kingdom are perhaps best seen in the characteristics of righteousness (Isa. 46:1; 51:5; 60:17, 21; 61:3, 11), obedience (Ps. 22:27; Jer. 31:33), holiness (Isa. 4:3–4; 35:8–10; Joel 3:17), truth (Ps. 85:10–11; Zech. 8:3), and the fullness of the Holy

Spirit (Joel 2:28–29).[8] Although these attributes are present today, in the millennial kingdom they will be intensified and expanded.

The clearest expression of the spiritual characteristics of the millennial kingdom is found in the worship and activity in the millennial temple. Jesus Christ will be reigning on the earth in Jerusalem and the millennial temple will be present and functioning as described in Ezekiel 40–46.

34. What happens at the end of the millennium?

At the end of the thousand-year reign of Christ on the earth, there will be one final rebellion by Satan and his forces. According to Revelation 20:7–10, Satan will be loosed at the end of the millennium and will rebel against the millennial reign of Christ. In one final grasp for power and human allegiance, Satan will manifest his true nature (as he has done throughout all of history) and attempt to seize the throne of God.

According to Revelation 20:10, Satan's termination will be swift and everlasting. He will be cast into the lake of fire joining the Antichrist and the False Prophet, who is the Antichrist's lieutenant (Rev. 13:11–18). The judgment of Satan is then followed by the judgment of the unbelieving dead, known as the great white throne judgment (Rev. 20:11–15). These judgments form the bridge between the millennium and the eternal state as described in Revelation 21–22. They are the final events of the millennium and conclude with the passing away of the present heavens and earth (Matt. 24:35; Mark 13:31; Luke 16:17; 21:33; 2 Peter 3:10).

35. Why does the millennium matter?

In a world filled with chaos, despair, corruption, violence, uncertainty, and rampant evil, the certainty of the millennium offers assurance that God's prophetic program has not been abandoned. Christ will rule the world with righteousness and justice. Evil will be judged and believers of all ages will worship Jesus Christ in His presence. God knows the future and controls the future. Because of this, Christians today need not have anxiety or fear from the head-lines. The "blessed hope" is Jesus Christ (Titus 2:13) and therefore Christians are to be active in these days before the Lord's return proclaiming the gospel of Jesus Christ (2 Cor. 5:11). We need not fear, for His kingdom will certainly come. We need to boldly pro-claim to all who will listen the saving message of our Lord and Savior Jesus Christ, the coming Messiah-King.

The magnificence of the millennium far exceeds anything we can imagine. Scripture gives us descriptive glimpses regarding the millennium but does not answer all of our questions. We know many things with certainty even though we do not know them completely. His kingdom will come and His will shall be done on the earth as it is in heaven. When this happens, the words of the hymnist will be fully realized:

> The sands of time are sinking,
> The dawn of heaven breaks;
> The summer morn I've sighed for,
> The fair sweet morn awakes.
> Dark, dark has been the midnight,
> But dayspring is at hand,
> And glory, glory dwelleth in
> Immanuel's land![9]

PART 6

What Does the Bible Teach About Heaven and the Eternal State?

Heaven is very real. In an age of fantasy, special effects, mysticism, and spiritual apathy, it's easy for heaven to be misrepresented. Yet, the Bible is very clear about the existence and purpose of heaven. Heaven and the eternal state are part of God's plan for the ages; therefore, heaven and prophecy are integrally related.[1]

36. Where does the Bible teach about heaven?

English translations of the Bible contain more than five hundred occurrences of the word *heaven*. Most of the verses use either the Hebrew word *shamayim,* which is literally translated "the heights," or the Greek word *ouranos,* which is literally translated "that which is raised up." These words are used throughout the Bible to refer to three different locations or realms: the atmosphere, the universe, and the abode of God. These three divisions have been recognized throughout history in both Christian and non-Christian sources, especially in classical Greek literature.[2] Although our concern is primarily the third usage, all three usages are common in the Bible.

1. *The atmospheric heaven.* Examples of this usage are seen in passages such as Deuteronomy 11:11, 17; 28:12, 24; Joshua 10:11; Psalms 18:13; 147:8; Proverbs 23:5; and Zechariah 2:6; 6:5. Verses such as these emphasize the "first heaven," or the atmospheric realm. It is of this realm that Isaiah speaks when he records God's words in Isaiah 55:9–11:

> For as the heavens are higher than the earth, so are My ways higher than your ways and My thoughts than your thoughts. For as the rain and the snow come down from heaven, and do not return there without watering the earth and making it bear and sprout, and furnishing seed to the sower and bread to the eater; so will My word be which goes forth from My mouth; it will not return to Me empty, without accomplishing what I desire, and without succeeding in the matter for which I sent it.

2. *The universe or celestial skies.* Examples of this usage are seen in passages such as Genesis 1:14; 15:5; Exodus 20:4; Psalm 33:6; Jeremiah 10:2; and Hebrews 1:10. Frequently, the celestial skies or heavens are used biblically in a figure of speech such as a hyperbole (Deut. 1:28; Dan. 4:11, 20, 22) or a metonymy, which emphasizes totality (Deut. 4:39; 30:19; Matt. 24:31; Col. 1:23). It is of this realm of the celestial skies and the totality of the universe that we read in Deuteronomy 30:19:

> I call heaven and earth to witness against you today, that I have set before you life and death, the blessing and the curse. So choose life in order that you may live, you and your descendants. . . .

It is also in this sense that we read of Jesus Christ's authority in Matthew 28:18–20:

> And Jesus came up and spoke to them, saying, "All authority has been given to Me in heaven and on earth. Go therefore and make disciples of all the nations, baptizing them in the name of the Father and the Son and the Holy Spirit, teaching them to observe all that I commanded you; and lo, I am with you always, even to the end of the age."

3. *The abode of God.* Examples of this usage are the primary focus of this study and are seen in passages such as Psalm 33:13–14; Isaiah 63:15; Matthew 5:16, 45; 6:1, 9; 7:11, 21; 18:10; and Revelation 3:12; 21:10. It is the abode of God that Jesus speaks of when He stated in Matthew 10:32–33:

> Therefore, everyone who confesses Me before men, I will also confess him before My Father who is in heaven. But whoever denies Me before men, I will also deny him before My Father who is in heaven.

It is the abode of God, the "third heaven" of which Paul speaks in 2 Corinthians 12:2. Jesus referred to heaven in this sense many times throughout His ministry.

Heaven is more than a mystical notion, an imaginary dreamland, or a philosophical concept. It is a real and present place in which God, the Creator of all things, lives. It is a place spoken of throughout the Bible. It is the true home of all Christians. It is where Jesus came from at the incarnation, where He ascended after the resurrection, and from whence He will come again to receive all of those who truly follow Him. It is the place that the writer of Hebrews calls a "better country" and for which those in the "hall of faith" longed (11:13–16).

37. Is there any difference between heaven and eternity?

When we talk about heaven, we are referring to a location or place. When we speak of eternity, we are talking about an era or eternal state. Heaven exists now even though we are not experiencing it. The eternal state is a yet-future dimension of time (without end). Heaven exists now and will continue to exist throughout eternity.

38. Where is heaven and does it exist now?

In Philippians 3:20, the apostle Paul writes to Christians stating "our citizenship is in heaven." Heaven is somewhere beyond earth and our universe. Heaven is in existence now and has been the dwelling place of God since eternity past. Heaven is the dwelling place of God, although He is not limited spatially to heaven because He is omnipresent. His omnipresence is reflected in Solomon's prayer at the dedication of the temple. "Behold, heaven and the highest heaven cannot contain You, how much less this house which I have built!" (1 Kings 8:27). In Psalm 139:8, the psalmist also speaks of God's omnipresence, stating, "If I ascend to heaven, You are there; if I make my bed in Sheol, behold, You are there." God's omnipresence does not limit Him to heaven, but heaven is His habitation. John MacArthur writes,

> So to say that God dwells in heaven is not to say that He is contained there. But it is uniquely His home, His center of operations, His command post. It is the place where His throne resides. And it's where the most perfect worship of Him occurs. It is in that sense that we say heaven is His dwelling-place.[3]

Although heaven is a place, it is not limited by physical boundaries or boundaries of time and space. It can be experienced and inhabited by beings with material bodies, but it is not restricted to things such as height and width and breadth. It has physical characteristics and attributes, but it is also extra-physical. MacArthur writes of heaven's attributes and uniqueness:

> So heaven is not confined to one locality marked off by boundaries that can be seen or measured. It transcends the confines of time-space dimensions. Perhaps that is part of what Scripture means when it states that God inhabits eternity (Isa. 57:15). His dwelling-place—heaven—is not subject to normal limitations of finite dimensions. We don't need to speculate about *how* this can be; it is sufficient to note that this is how Scripture describes heaven. It is a real place where people with physical bodies will dwell in God's presence for all eternity; and it is also a realm that surpasses our finite concept of what a "place" is.[4]

Although it is very real, heaven may be nonspatial in its present intermediate state. It is the place where Christ is now, but it is also beyond our normal senses and experiences. It is truly a supernatural phenomenon.

39. When does the eternal state or eternity begin?

According to Revelation 21 and 22, the eternal state will begin at the end of the millennium, the thousand-year reign of Christ on the earth. From our current point in history, the next event in God's prophetic plan is the rapture of the church, which will be followed by the seven-year tribulation, the second coming of Christ, the millennial kingdom, and, finally, the eternal state.

Eternity is distinct from the millennial kingdom. During the millennium, Jesus Christ will rule on the earth for one thousand years. At the end of this period, there will be a series of judgments and the ushering in of the eternal state.

40. What will take place in heaven?

The Bible describes life in heaven as full of joy, purposeful activity, and worship. When we think of eternity, it's easy to wonder if we will get bored in heaven. However, the biblical glimpses are not of boredom. The Bible speaks of at least six activities in heaven: worship, service, authority and administration, fellowship, learning, and rest.[5]

1. *Worship without distraction.* Worship will be the primary activity in heaven. Some of the most extensive passages on worship in heaven are found in Revelation 4–5 and 19:1–8. On the basis of Revelation 4:8–11, the worship of God in heaven can be seen to include at least six things:
   • A celebration of God's greatness (v. 8).
   • A celebration of God's goodness (v. 9).
   • A submission before God's sovereignty (v. 10).
   • An adoration of God's person (v. 10).
   • A self-renunciation before God's glory (v. 10).
   • An exaltation of God's name (v. 11).[6]

2. *Service without exhaustion.* In Revelation 22:3 we read, "There will no longer be any curse; and the throne of God and of the Lamb will be in it, and His bond-servants will serve Him." Throughout Revelation, the phrase *bond-servant* is used to describe those who are in heaven and experiencing its glories. Unlike the current work, future service to God in heaven will be without time demands, without frustration, without fear of failure, without limitations, and without exhaustion. It will come from worship and motivation that is pure, and it will be a joyful experience.

3. *Administration without failure.* In Revelation 22:5, we read that believers in heaven shall "reign forever and ever." In Luke 19:17 and 19, Jesus taught that in the future reward and authority would be given to those who followed Him. He

also indicated that the authority and administration would include judgment over the twelve tribes of Israel (Matt. 19:28; Luke 22:30). In 1 Corinthians 6:3, Paul states that Christians will also have authority over the angels in heaven.

4. *Fellowship without suspicion.* Heaven will provide believers of all ages with the opportunity for limitless fellowship with each other and with Jesus Christ (Matt. 8:11; Rev. 19:9). In heaven we will fellowship with both those Christians we knew on the earth, as well as with Old Testament saints and those Christians who lived before and after us, and with those whom present circumstances have not allowed us to know.

5. *Learning without weariness.* Only God is omniscient, but in heaven there will finally be the opportunity and the time to know all that we want to know and to have answers to all of the questions and mysteries of life that are so perplexing in this world. Our capacity to learn will be limitless. We will be able to say with the apostle Paul "then I will know fully just as I also have been fully known." (1 Cor. 13:12).

6. *Rest without boredom.* Revelation 14:10–13 contrasts the eternal destiny of the righteous and the unrighteous. In verse 11, the unrighteous are said to have "no rest" in contrast to the righteous, who will "rest from their labors, for their deeds follow with them" (v. 13). There will be no fatigue or exhaustion. In heaven, we will be fully satisfied, and the words of David the psalmist will be fully realized by those who are God's own: "As for me, I shall behold Your face in righteousness; I will be satisfied with Your likeness when I awake" (Ps. 17:15).

41. How can I be sure I will go to heaven?

Theologian Carl F. H. Henry wrote of contemporary society and its citizens, "The intellectual suppression of God in His revelation has precipitated the bankruptcy of a civilization that turned its back on heaven only to make its bed in hell."[7] Is this bold but true statement an accurate reflection of your own spiritual status?

Perhaps you have reached this final question in this booklet and yet do not know for sure what will be your eternal destiny. If so, then this is the most important question of the book for you, and we encourage you to consider carefully its answer.

We would like you to know for sure that you have eternal life through Jesus Christ, God's Son. In Revelation, the closing book of the Bible, John issues a last invitation: "The Spirit and the bride say, 'Come.' And let the one who hears say, 'Come.' And let the one who is thirsty come; let the one who wishes take the water of life without cost" (Rev. 22:17). What does this invitation mean?

The image is that of a wedding. The groom has issued an invitation to the bride. The groom is willing, but is the bride willing? In this same way, God has made provision for you—at no expense to you, but at great expense to Him—to enter into a relationship with Him that will give you eternal life. More specifically, the invitation is issued to the one who hears and who is thirsty. *Thirst* represents a need: forgiveness of sin. Thus, you must recognize that you are a sinner in the eyes of God: "For all have sinned and fall short of the glory of God" (Rom. 3:23). God is holy and thus cannot ignore anyone's sin. He must judge it. However, God in His mercy has provided a way by which sinful men and women can receive His forgiveness. This forgiveness was provided at a great cost by Jesus Christ when He came to the earth two thousand years ago, lived a perfect life, and died on the cross in our place to pay for our sin: "For the wages of sin is death, but the free gift of God is eternal life in Christ Jesus our Lord" (Rom. 6:23). The Bible also says, "Christ died for our sins according to the Scriptures, and that He was buried, and that He was raised on the third day according to the Scriptures" (1 Cor. 15:3–4).

To obtain this salvation and the eternal life that Jesus Christ offers, we must individually trust that Christ's payment through

His death on the cross is the only way that we can receive the forgiveness of our sins, the re-establishment of a relationship with God, and eternal life. "For by grace you have been saved through faith; and that not of yourselves, it is the gift of God; not as a result of works, so that no one may boast" (Eph. 2:8–9). This is why John invites the thirsty to come and enter into a relationship with God through Christ.

Are you thirsty? Do you recognize your sin before God? If you do, then come to Christ. If you do not acknowledge your need for salvation, then you bypass this opportunity. Please don't.

Those who are thirsty and want salvation can express their trust through the following prayer:

> Dear Lord, I know that I have done wrong and fallen short of Your perfect ways. I realize that my sins have separated me from You and that I deserve Your judgment. I believe that You sent Your Son, Jesus Christ, to earth to die on the cross for my sins. I put my trust in Jesus Christ and what He did on the cross as payment for my sins. Please forgive me and give me eternal life. Amen.

If you just prayed this prayer in sincerity, you are now a child of God and have eternal life. Heaven will be your eternal home. Welcome to the family of God! As His child, you will want to develop this wonderful relationship by learning more about God through study of the Bible. You will want to find a church that teaches God's Word, encourages fellowship with other believers, and promotes the spreading of God's message of forgiveness to others.

If you were a Christian before reading this book, we encourage you to continue in your relationship with Christ. As you grow, you will want to live for Him in light of His coming. You will want to continue to spread the message of forgiveness that you have experienced. As you see God setting the stage for the end-time drama of events, you should be motivated to increased service until He comes.

Heaven is indeed a unique and wonderful place, a location that far exceeds our imagination and comprehension. For the Christian, it is a present hope and eternal home. The decision you make about heaven and the free offer of salvation based on the death of Jesus Christ is the most important decision you will ever make. Take care of your soul; you will have it for eternity.

Notes

Part 1: What Is Bible Prophecy?

1. Walter Kaiser, *Back Toward the Future: Hints for Interpreting Biblical Prophecy* (Grand Rapids: Baker, 1989), 20.
2. Ibid., 21.
3. Kenneth Gentry, Jr., *He Shall Have Dominion: A Postmillennial Eschatology* (Tyler, TX: Institute for Christian Economics, 1992), 148, 146.
4. *Webster's New Twentieth Century Dictionary,* Unabridged, Second Edition, s.v. "literal."
5. Paul Lee Tan, *The Interpretation of Prophecy* (Winona Lake, IN: Assurance, 1974), 29.
6. Roy B. Zuck, *Basic Bible Interpretation: A Practical Guide to Discovering Biblical Truth* (Wheaton, IL: Victor, 1991), 100.
7. Ibid., 100–101.
8. Tan, *Interpretation of Prophecy,* 103.
9. Zuck, *Basic Bible Interpretation,* 77.
10. David L. Cooper, *The World's Greatest Library: Graphically Illustrated* (Los Angeles: Biblical Research Society, 1970), 11.
11. Elliott E. Johnson, *Expository Hermeneutics: An Introduction* (Grand Rapids: Zondervan, 1990), 9.
12. Charles C. Ryrie, *Basic Theology: A Popular Systematic Guide to Understanding Biblical Truth* (Wheaton, IL: Victor, 1986), 450.

13. Philip Schaff, *History of the Christian Church*, reprint ed., 3rd ed., vol. 2 (Peabody, MA: Hendrickson, 2006), 614.

14. Ryrie, *Basic Theology*, 449.

15. John F. Walvoord, *The Millennial Kingdom* (Findlay, OH: Dunham, 1959), 23.

16. See Rodney Clapp, "Democracy as Heresy," *Christianity Today*, 20 February 1987, 18–19; and Gary North, ed. "Apologetics and Strategy," *Tactics of Christian Resistance* (Tyler, TX: Geneva Ministries, 1983), 107. For a fuller critique of Christian Reconstructionism, see H. Wayne House and Thomas Ice, *Dominion Theology: Blessing or Curse?* (Portland, OR: Multnomah, 1988).

17. For a fuller refutation of preterism, see Tim LaHaye and Thomas Ice, eds., *The End Times Controversy: The Second Coming Under Attack* (Eugene, OR: Harvest House, 2003); and Mark Hitchcock and Thomas Ice, *Breaking the Apocalypse Code: Setting the Record Straight About the End Times* (Costa Mesa, CA: The Word for Today, 2007).

18. On this passage and the interpretation of it, see Thomas Ice, "The Olivet Discourse," in LaHaye and Ice, *End Times Controversy*, 151–200.

19. For a more detailed rebuttal of this view, see Mark Hitchcock, "The Stake in the Heart: The AD 95 Date of Revelation," in LaHaye and Ice, *End Times Controversy*, 123–50. This issue was also the subject of Hitchcock's PhD dissertation "A Defense of the Domitianic Date of the Book of Revelation," (Dallas Theological Seminary, 2005).

20. Irenaeus, *Against Heresies* 5.30.3.

21. See Hitchcock, "The Stake in the Heart," in LaHaye and Ice, *End Times Controversy*, 123–50. In this chapter Hitchcock addresses early writers such as Hegesippus, Irenaeus, Statius, Clement of Alexandria, Tertullian, Eusebius and others. More detailed analysis regarding Polycarp and other Fathers is found in Hitchcock's PhD dissertation "A Defense of the Domitianic Date of the Book of Revelation," cited above.

22. Eusebius, *Historia Ecclesiae*, III, 18; *Chron. ad an. Abrahami*, 2110.

23. For a more extensive discussion of the date of Revelation, see Hitchcock, "The Stake in the Heart," in LaHaye and Ice, *End Times Controversy*.

24. For an expansion of these ideas, see Thomas Ice, "Some Practical Dangers of Preterism," in LaHaye and Ice, *End Times Controversy*, 419–29.

25. Kenneth L. Gentry, Jr., "A Preterist View of Revelation" in *Four Views on the Book of Revelation*, ed. C. Marvin Pate (Grand Rapids: Zondervan, 1998), 87.

26. For an explanation of the Hindu concept of *Maya*, see John B. Noss, *Man's Religions*, 5th ed. (New York: Macmillan, 1974), 99, 197, 199, 229.

27. Gary North, "Publisher's Preface" in *Before Jerusalem Fell* by Kenneth L. Gentry Jr. (Tyler, TX: Institute for Christian Economics, 1989), xi.

28. Gentry, "A Preterist View of Revelation," 86–89.

29. Ibid.

30. See Thomas Ice, "The Olivet Discourse," in LaHaye and Ice, *End Times Controversy*, 151–200.

31. Arnold Fruchtenbaum, "Israel and the Church" in *Issues in Dispensationalism*, ed. Wesley Willis, John Master, and Charles Ryrie (Chicago: Moody Press, 1994), 129.

32. Ibid., 113.

33. Ibid., 113–15.

34. Ibid., 116.

35. Ibid., 116–18.

36. Ibid., 117–18.

37. Carl F. H. Henry, *God, Revelation, and Authority*, vol. 3 (Waco, TX: Word, 1976), 24.

38. Carl F. H. Henry, *New Strides of Faith* (Chicago: Moody Press, 1972), 133. Emphasis in original.

Part 2: What Does the Bible Teach About the Rapture?

1. *Dictionary of New Testament Theology*, s.v. "Snatch," by C. Brown, 3:602.
2. Renald Showers, *Maranatha: Our Lord, Come!* (Bellmawr, NJ: The Friends of Israel Gospel Ministry, 1995), 127–28.

Part 3: What Does the Bible Teach About the Tribulation?

1. For a more thorough treatment of these passages, see J. Randall Price, "Old Testament Tribulation Terms," in *When the Trumpet Sounds*, ed. Thomas Ice and Timothy Demy (Eugene, OR: Harvest House, 1995), 57–84.
2. Arnold G. Fruchtenbaum, *The Footsteps of the Messiah: A Study of the Sequence of Prophetic Events* (San Antonio: Ariel Press, 1982, rev. ed. 2003), 122–26.
3. Ibid., 123, 124.
4. Ibid., 125.
5. We are following events as outlined by Fruchtenbaum in *Footsteps of the Messiah*, 135–91.
6. See the following presentations of this view: Gary DeMar, *Last Days Madness: Obsession of the Modern Church* (Powder Springs, GA: American Vision, 1999), 414–16; Gary DeMar, "A Review of *The Remnant*," http://www.preteristsite.com /docs/demarremnant.html (accessed August 18, 2010).
7. Fruchtenbaum, *Footsteps of the Messiah*, 125–26.
8. DeMar, "A Review of *The Remnant*."
9. Fruchtenbaum, *Footsteps of the Messiah*, 345.
10. One of the most readable and extensive discussions on the chronology of the seventy weeks is found in Harold H. Hoehner, *Chronological Aspects of the Life of Christ* (Grand Rapids: Zondervan, 1977), 115–39. A more popular presentation is Herb Vander Lugt, *The Daniel Papers* (Grand Rapids: Radio Bible Class, 1994).

11. Hoehner, *Chronological Aspects,* 139.

12. An earlier version of the answer to this question, answered by Tim, appeared in *The Popular Encyclopedia of Bible Prophecy,* ed. Tim LaHaye and Ed Hindson (Eugene, OR: Harvest House, 2004), 203–5.

13. Grant Osborne, *Revelation* (Grand Rapids: Baker, 2002), 517.

14. Robert H. Mounce, *The Book of Revelation* (Grand Rapids: Eerdmans, 1977), 262.

15. Robert L. Thomas, *Revelation 8–22: An Exegetical Commentary* (Chicago: Moody Press, 1995), 183.

16. Osborne, *Revelation,* 519–20.

17. Thomas, *Revelation 8–22,* 184–85, 187–88.

18. Fruchtenbaum, *Footsteps of the Messiah*, 205.

19. Osborne, *Revelation,* 518–19.

20. One of the most thorough studies of the events of Armageddon is Fruchtenbaum's *Footsteps of the Messiah,* 216–53. See also, Thomas Ice and Timothy Demy, *The Truth About Armageddon and the Middle East* (Eugene, OR: Harvest House, 1997).

21. See Fruchtenbaum, *Footsteps of the Messiah*, 256–63 for a full discussion of this interval.

Part 4: What Does the Bible Teach About the Second Coming?

1. John F. Walvoord, *Major Bible Prophecies: 37 Crucial Prophecies That Affect You Today* (Grand Rapids: Zondervan, 1991), 390.

2. Carl F. H. Henry, *Carl Henry at His Best* (Portland, OR: Multnomah, 1989), 127–28.

Part 5: What Does the Bible Teach About the Millennium?

1. John F. Walvoord, *Prophecy: 14 Essential Keys to Understanding the Final Drama* (Nashville: Thomas Nelson, 1993), 139.

2. J. Dwight Pentecost, *Things to Come: A Study in Biblical Eschatology* (Grand Rapids: Zondervan, 1958), 563–79.

3. Charles C. Ryrie, *Basic Theology: A Popular Systematic Guide to Understanding Biblical Truth* (Wheaton, IL: Victor, 1986), 511.

4. David L. Larsen, *Jews, Gentiles, and the Church: A New Perspective on History and Prophecy* (Grand Rapids: Discovery House, 1995), 316.

5. John F. Walvoord, *Major Bible Prophecies: 37 Crucial Prophecies That Affect You Today* (Grand Rapids: Zondervan, 1991), 331.

6. Arnold G. Fruchtenbaum, *The Footsteps of the Messiah: A Study of the Sequence of Prophetic Events* (San Antonio: Ariel Press, 1982, rev. ed. 2003), 256–63.

7. Paul Benware, *Understanding End Times Prophecy: A Comprehensive Approach* (Chicago: Moody Press, 1995), 284.

8. Pentecost, *Things to Come,* 482–87.

9. Anne R. Cousin, "The Sands of Time Are Sinking," 1857.

Part 6: What Does the Bible Teach About Heaven and the Eternal State?

1. For a fuller discussion of heaven and eternity, see the authors' work in this same series *Answers to Common Questions About Heaven and Eternity.*

2. For examples from classical literature, see Wilbur M. Smith, *The Biblical Doctrine of Heaven* (Chicago: Moody Press, 1968), 28–29.

3. John F. MacArthur, *The Glory of Heaven* (Wheaton, IL: Crossway, 1996), 56.

4. Ibid., 60.

5. See Smith, *Biblical Doctrine of Heaven,* 199–200; Don Baker, *Heaven: A Glimpse of Your Future Home* (Portland, OR: Multnomah, 1983); and Douglas Connelly, *After Life: What the Bible Really Says* (Downers Grove, IL: InterVarsity Press, 1995), 101–3.

6. Steven J. Lawson, *Heaven Help Us! Truths About Eternity That Will Help You Live Today* (Colorado Springs: NavPress, 1995), 52–66.

7. Carl F. H. Henry, *Twilight of a Great Civilization* (Westchester, IL: Crossway, 1988), 143.

Recommended Reading

Benware, Paul. *Understanding End Times Prophecy: A Comprehensive Approach*. Chicago: Moody Press, 1995.

Fruchtenbaum, Arnold G. *The Footsteps of the Messiah: A Study of the Sequence of Prophetic Events*. Tustin, CA: Ariel Ministries, 1982, rev. ed. 2003.

Hitchcock, Mark. *101 Answers to the Most Asked Questions About the End Times*. Sisters, OR: Multnomah, 2001.

_____. *The Complete Book of Bible Prophecy*. Wheaton, IL: Tyndale, 1999.

Hitchcock, Mark and Thomas Ice. *Breaking the Apocalypse Code: Setting the Record Straight About the End Times*. Costa Mesa, CA: The Word for Today, 2007.

Hoehner, Harold H. *Chronological Aspects of the Life of Christ*. Grand Rapids: Zondervan, 1977.

House, H. Wayne and Thomas Ice. *Dominion Theology: Blessing or Curse? An Analysis of Christian Reconstructionism*. Portland, OR: Multnomah, 1988.

Ice, Thomas and Timothy Demy. *The Truth About Armageddon and the Middle East*. Eugene, OR: Harvest House, 1997.

Ice, Thomas and Timothy Demy, eds. *When the Trumpet Sounds: Today's Foremost Authorities Speak Out on End-Time Controversies*. Eugene, OR, Harvest House, 1995.

Johnson, Elliott E. *Expository Hermeneutics: An Introduction*. Grand Rapids: Zondervan, 1990.

Kaiser, Walter. *Back Toward the Future: Hints for Interpreting Biblical Prophecy*. Grand Rapids: Baker, 1989.

LaHaye, Tim and Ed Hindson, eds. *The Popular Encyclopedia of Bible Prophecy*. Eugene, OR: Harvest House, 2004.

LaHaye, Tim and Thomas Ice. *Charting the End Times*. Eugene, OR: Harvest House, 2001.

LaHaye, Tim and Thomas Ice, eds. *The End Times Controversy: The Second Coming Under Attack*. Eugene, OR: Harvest House, 2003.

Larsen, David L. *Jews, Gentiles, and the Church: A New Perspective on History and Prophecy*. Grand Rapids: Discovery House, 1995.

MacArthur, John F. *The Glory of Heaven*. Wheaton, IL: Crossway, 1996.

Pentecost, J. Dwight. *Things to Come: A Study in Biblical Eschatology*. Grand Rapids: Zondervan, 1958.

Price, Randall. *The Coming Last Days Temple*. Eugene, OR: Harvest House, 1999.

_____. *Jerusalem in Prophecy: God's Stage for the Final Drama*. Eugene, OR: Harvest House, 1998.

Ryrie, Charles C. *Basic Theology: A Popular Systematic Guide to Understanding Biblical Truth*. Wheaton, IL: Victor Books, 1986.

Showers, Renald. *Maranatha: Our Lord, Come!* Bellmawr, NJ: The Friends of Israel Gospel Ministry, 1995.

Smith, Wilbur M. *The Biblical Doctrine of Heaven*. Chicago: Moody Press, 1968.

Tan, Paul Lee. *The Interpretation of Prophecy*. Winona Lake, IN: Assurance, 1974.

Thomas, Robert L. *Revelation 1–7: An Exegetical Commentary*. Chicago: Moody Press, 1992.

_____. *Revelation 8–22: An Exegetical Commentary*. Chicago: Moody Press, 1995.

Walvoord, John F. *The Blessed Hope and the Tribulation*. Grand
        Rapids: Zondervan, 1976.
_____. *Daniel: The Key to Prophetic Revelation*. Chicago: Moody
        Press, 1971.
_____. *Major Bible Prophecies: 37 Crucial Prophecies That Affect
        You Today*. Grand Rapids: Zondervan, 1991.
_____. *The Millennial Kingdom*. Findlay, OH: Dunham, 1959.
_____. *Prophecy: 14 Essential Keys to Understanding the Final
        Drama*. Nashville: Thomas Nelson, 1993.
_____. *The Rapture Question*. Grand Rapids: Zondervan [1957],
        1979.
_____. *The Return of the Lord*. Grand Rapids: Zondervan, 1955.
Zuck, Roy B. *Basic Bible Interpretation: A Practical Guide to Discov-
        ering Biblical Truth*. Wheaton, IL: Victor Books, 1991.

About the Authors

Timothy J. Demy has authored and edited more than two dozen books on Bible, theology, and current issues. He has also contributed to numerous journals, Bible handbooks, study Bibles, and theological encyclopedias. A professor of military ethics at the US Naval War College, he served more than twenty-seven years as a military chaplain in a variety of assignments afloat and ashore with the US Navy, US Marine Corps, and US Coast Guard. He has published and spoken nationally and internationally on issues of war and peace and the role of religion in international relations. He also serves as an adjunct professor of systematic theology at Baptist Bible Seminary.

In addition to his theological training, which he received at Dallas Theological Seminary (ThM, ThD), Dr. Demy received the MSt in international relations from the University of Cambridge and MA and PhD degrees from Salve Regina University, where he wrote about C. S. Lewis. He also earned graduate degrees in European history and in national security and strategic studies and was the President's Honor Graduate from the US Naval War College.

He is a member of numerous professional organizations, including the Evangelical Theological Society, the Society of Biblical Literature, and is Fellow of the Royal Society of Arts (UK). He and his wife, Lyn, have been married thirty-two years.

Thomas Ice is Executive Director of the Pre-Trib Research Center in Lynchburg, Virginia, which he founded in 1994 with Dr. Tim LaHaye to research, teach, and defend the pretribulational rapture and related Bible prophecy doctrines. He is also an Associate Professor of Systematic Theology at Liberty University and Seminary. Dr. Ice has authored and coauthored more than thirty books, written hundreds of articles, and contributed to several study Bibles and theological encyclopedias. He is a frequent national and international conference speaker on topics in prophecy and theology. He served as a pastor for fifteen years prior to his present ministry. Dr. Ice has a BA from Howard Payne University, a ThM from Dallas Theological Seminary, and a PhD from Tyndale Theological Seminary; he is also a PhD candidate at the University of Wales. He is a member of several professional organizations including the Evangelical Theological Society. He lives with his wife, Janice, in Lynchburg, Virginia, and they have three grown sons.